Orson Welles

By the same author:

Woody Allen
Hong Kong's Heroic Bloodshed (Editor)

Writing as Paul Duncan:

Film Noir
Alfred Hitchcock
Stanley Kubrick
Noir Fiction
Martin Scorsese

Orson Welles

Martin Fitzgerald

www.pocketessentials.com

Third edition published in 2010 by Pocket Essentials

P.O. Box 394, Harpenden, Herts, AL5 1XJ

www.pocketessentials.com

ISBN 978-1-84243- 286-0

2 4 6 8 10 9 7 5 3 1

Typeset by Avocet Typeset, Chilton, Aylesbury, Bucks
Printed and bound in Great Britain by Cox & Wyman, Reading

For Claude and Josef

Acknowledgements

My thanks to Ellen Cheshire, John Ashbrook, Simon Bloom and Cinematheek Eindhoven for providing research materials.

Contents

1. Orson Welles: Labyrinth Without a Centre   11
2. *Citizen Kane* (1941)   30
3. *The Magnificent Ambersons* (1942)   44
4. *The Stranger* (1946)   53
5. *The Lady from Shanghai* (1948)   59
6. *Macbeth* (1948)   69
7. *Othello* (1952)   78
8. *Mr Arkadin* (1955)   88
9. *Touch of Evil* (1958)   100
10. *The Trial* (1963)   114
11. *Chimes at Midnight* (1965)   126
12. *The Immortal Story* (1968)   135
13. *F for Fake* (1973)   138
14. *Filming Othello* (1978)   146
15. Lost Films   148
Resource Materials   151
Index   157

Orson Welles: Labyrinth Without a Centre

'Envy is a desire of having, and jealousy is the pain or fear of losing.'

During the 1942 Oscar ceremony, *Citizen Kane* was up for nine awards. Each time a nomination for *Citizen Kane* was announced, amongst the ripples of polite applause, there could be heard booing, hissing and derisive laughter. Who could blame them? Two years earlier Orson Welles, then a mere boy of 24, had walked into Hollywood, been given all the money and resources he could possibly need, and made a great film. Shooting a film was 'the biggest electric train set any boy ever had', Welles had said. In making *Citizen Kane*, he had shown more vitality, invention and showmanship than 90% of the assembled Hollywood veterans could ever hope to achieve. The reason for their booing was obvious – they were jealous. And they were determined to make sure Welles never got to play with his train set again.

'Promises are more fun than explanations.'

1999 was an extraordinary year for Orson Welles.

April 1999 saw the premiere of George Hickenlooper's political drama *The Big Brass Ring*, which was scripted by Orson Welles and his companion Oja Kodar in the early 1980s.

Tim Robbins' film *Cradle Will Rock* premiered in Cannes on 18 May 1999 and was released in the US in December. It detailed the controversial events surrounding Welles' 1937 stage production of Marc Blitzstein's musical *The Cradle Will Rock*. The government prevented this left-wing play from being shown and the union banned actors from performing it on stage. After the armed servicemen occupied the New York theatre on 15 June 1937, the cast, crew and audience walked to another theatre, where the actors performed in the audience so they did not break union rules. It was a tremendously vital moment in time.

According to many, *Citizen Kane* was Welles' greatest film. If people complained about anything else he made (and, believe me, they did), at least Welles had *Citizen Kane*. They could never take that away from him. *RKO 281* is a film about the making of *Citizen Kane*. Directed by Benjamin Ross, filmed in the UK and featuring a great cast (John Malkovich, Roy Scheider, James Cromwell, Melanie Griffith, David Suchet, Brenda Blethyn), it premiered on American cable TV on 20 November 1999. Like *Cradle Will Rock*, *RKO 281* is not an accurate portrayal of events, but a careful distortion. The truth has been re-engineered to give Welles relationships with two older men – writer Herman J Mankiewicz and newspaper tycoon William Randolph Hearst. (The young man quarrelling with the old one was a theme running through all Welles' movies, and it is a clever idea to utilise it here.)

The main failure of both films is that Welles does not emerge as a larger-than-life personality, someone who can be achingly funny one moment and throwing a tantrum the next. He is presented as part of a tableau, not the centre of attention or a prime mover. In life, Welles was tall. He had presence when he entered a room. As Hilton Edwards once said of him, 'He had a wonderful capacity for displacing air.'

Then a re-edited and restored version of Welles' film noir masterpiece, *Touch of Evil* (1958), was released in the UK in 1999 to great acclaim. During the making of the film, Welles dictated a 58-page memo outlining edits he would like to make using the existing footage. About half were included. Forty years later, the other half were carefully inserted by Walter Murch. The subtle edits make important changes to the rhythm and tone of the movie. It is the closest we are ever likely to get to how Welles envisaged the film.

The evening of Christmas Day 1999 saw a Welles triple bill on British TV – the premiere of *RKO 281*, followed by *Citizen Kane* and *The Trial*. It is extraordinary that a filmmaker who is generally perceived as a failed artist, as a man who went downhill after *Citizen Kane* in 1941, should now command so much respect and critical attention.

What does Welles have that people still want? This book is an attempt to investigate what lies at the centre of that labyrinth.

Fat Man or Genius?

'Everybody denies that I am a genius – but nobody ever called me one.'

Welles is often portrayed as some sort of tragic figure. In the anorexic age, a fat man is seen as visually sad. Welles was in no way sad – he was a great raconteur and lover of life. He did not dwell on the past, but lived for the future and the next movie or three he was in the process of making.

People point to Welles' sherry adverts as a sign of his decline. This is a preposterous idea because throughout his career his voice and acting skills were for hire to whoever paid the most. The money was used to pay bills or finance a film project.

It has often been said that Welles wasted his talent. How? By writing and directing some of the most powerful and memorable American film, theatre and radio productions ever made? Allied to this notion of waste is the idea that Welles started at the top and worked his way down. It implies that his later work was somehow less, that Welles was a worse storyteller, that he did not concern himself with proper subjects. This is blatantly untrue, as I hope you will understand when you finish reading this book.

When critics and academics discuss Welles there is something in the air, an emotion, which is difficult to pin down. It is disappointment. Everybody knows he was a great filmmaker, and he proved it time and time again, yet people still moan and groan over the films that might have been. Why do people concentrate so much on works that do not exist?

My humble opinion is that lovers of film love Welles. His work is full of joy, of excitement. He is a big kid showing his adopted parents (us, the viewers) his latest toy. He is three-year-old Georgie Welles writing, producing, directing and acting all the parts of his puppet theatre. He is the school-kid telling his classmates ghost stories at night. He is the practised magician, cajoling and tricking his audience, a look of bemusement on his face when the trick goes right. He is the serious young man, apologetic for frightening America by pretending aliens had landed, explaining he was unaware that stories had this sort of effect on people.

So when Welles died with so many films unfinished, I genuinely believe that this air of disappointment, of unfulfilled promise, is a kind of compliment. What people are saying is that they loved his movies so much that they wanted to see more.

And then, out of frustration, people try to apportion blame. Why did Welles not finish his films? Well, it was not for a lack of trying. He hired out his voice to radio and commercials, his acting ability to good and bad films alike, his presence to TV talk shows, to gain the funds to film another 20 minutes of *Othello* or another five minutes of *The Other Side of the Wind*. Welles never had the consistent support of one studio or producer. He was never in demand as a commercial director. He was only wanted as an actor.

Furthermore, people began resenting Welles, feeling somehow that he owed them those lost films. We are raised in a capitalist culture, which says that if there is a demand, a supply will come into being. Deep down, we think of a film as a product to be consumed, that the makers of films will go right ahead and build one for us if we wish. This was the case in Hollywood in 1939, when Welles began his career in film. The studio was a production line, cranking out A-films, B-films, shorts, newsreels and cartoons to fill the enormous demand for product. The only problem with this idea was that Welles did not want to make the type of films that hordes of people wanted to see.

He was an artist who wanted to make films that meant something to him personally. And when the Hollywood film studios decided to stop financing these personal statements, Welles went out and financed them himself, becoming one of America's first independent filmmakers at a time when the concept did not even exist.

Playing with the Train Set

'There are a thousand ways of playing a good classic. If it were effective, I would play Hamlet on a trapeze.'

Sounds crash loudly. There is silence. A blinding light is shining at us, then it is dark. We hear a whisper, then overlapping dialogue. What is going on!!?

You cannot passively watch an Orson Welles film. He demands that you participate in some way. It is as though Welles is saying, 'Either pay attention, or get out of my theatre!' And theatre is the operative word here. Welles came from a theatre experience that demanded he grab the audience from the first second and keep them gasping until the curtain went down.

Welles transferred what he learnt in the theatre to the silver screen. *Doctor Faustus*, which premiered in New York on 8 January 1937, starred the 21-year-old Welles in his first major stage role. He also directed and John Houseman produced. The critics loved it. The audience loved it. It was innovative because the bare stage was defined by areas of light. The type and amount of light on the characters told the audience the place, time and relationship between the characters. Welles reused this idea in *The Magnificent Ambersons* and other films – characters talking to each other surrounded by blackness. This effect was helped by Welles' use of deep-focus photography, which allows close and distant characters to be in focus at the same time. Expressionistic lighting distorts and reveals character. Expressionism is showing the internal thoughts and feelings of a person or object in an external way. Once you realise that Orson Welles grew up at the height of Expressionism in the 1930s, the manner of his performances and the style of his direction suddenly make sense.

For sound, Welles also went deep focus; you can tell if a person is near or far away by the quality of the sound. In addition, he used overlapping dialogue, with several characters talking at the same time. Welles was able to achieve this because of his work in radio. When he was living from hand to mouth in New York with his first wife Virginia, he decided to try *The March of Time* (a news magazine which recreated events) and he was taken on because he could imitate the voice of any famous person they needed. Welles became a regular (working with Agnes

Moorehead, Jeanette Nolan, Ted de Corsica, Ray Collins and Paul Stewart) and learned about timing, overlapping dialogue and integrating himself into a sound collage. Although not credited, he was known throughout the industry and renowned for turning up and reading his scripts 'cold', i.e. without a rehearsal.

Then there is the movement of a story: how the images are edited together; the introductory and linking voiceover; how the image is framed whilst the camera is both still and moving, and so on. Welles, sitting in front of a moviola, expressed it best in *Filming Othello*: '(Thomas) Carlyle said that almost everything examined deeply enough will turn out to be musical. Of course this is profoundly true of motion pictures. The pictures have movement; the movies move. Then there's the movement from one picture to another. There's a rhythmic structuring to that; there's counterpoint, harmony and dissonance. A film is never right, until it's right musically. This moviola, this filmmaker's tool, is a kind of a musical instrument.'

And what of the space within which this movement takes place? Welles loved to sketch, to design the environment, the sets and the costumes, because it reflected the feeling and mood he was trying to create. It is all part of the final image. There are many stories of Welles staying up all night to paint the sets himself. Welles even designed the decor and costumes for a ballet (*The Lady in the Ice*) in 1953.

These were all storytelling tools that Welles learned to use, but to what end? What ideas were in his head? What was he trying to say?

Rosebud

'Don't ask for the meaning, ask for the use.' – Ludwig
Wittgenstein

Welles said he told stories and wanted the audience to
work out for themselves what it was all about. After
looking at his films, it becomes apparent that certain ideas
and themes are repeated.

For all his exuberance of style and presentation, there is
something innately sad about Welles' work. His films are
about the end of things. Often beginning with a death, we
learn about the life of one or more characters. We learn a
little about their rise, but mostly about their fall. We experience their betrayal, their loss of innocence and integrity.
We are shown people losing all they hold dear. *Citizen
Kane*, *Othello*, *Mr Arkadin* and *Touch of Evil* all begin with
a death. In his seven other fiction films the central char-
acter(s) die(s) at the end.

The stories are all devices for finding out the truth
about people, about what is inside them, what makes them
tick. Charles Foster Kane needs an audience and desperately wants to be loved by them. George Minafer has the
love of his mother and will do everything in his power to
prevent her giving any of it away to Eugene Morgan.
Michael O'Hara loves lost causes, including the Spanish
Civil War and Elsa Bannister. Macbeth will do anything to
obtain power but does not know what to do with it when
he gets it. All the doubts and fears within Othello – his
colour, his class, his potency in bed – are unleashed by
Iago with tragic results. For all his power, Arkadin only

wants to be loved by his daughter. For all his detection skills, Hank Quinlan could not find his wife's killer and it haunts him, driving him to use any means necessary to solve future murders. Although Joseph K portrays himself as being oppressed by society, he is also an oppressor. Falstaff only wants to be loved by Prince Hal. Impotent Mr Clay wants to prove he still has power over people.

We find out the truth through the relationship between a man of power and a man of integrity. Thus, the contrast is shown between Charles and Jedediah, Hal and Falstaff, and Quinlan and Menzies. There are variations to this relationship with Othello and Iago, and Arkadin and Van Stratten.

Biographers have speculated about the origins of these themes. Some say that they are personal. It is very tempting to read Welles as Kane or George Minafer, but it is essentially a pointless exercise since we will never know for sure. Welles himself makes the point in *F for Fake* that a) you should never believe experts and b) a work is either a piece of art or it is not, regardless of who made it and under which circumstances.

Welles' preoccupation with death is intriguing and understandable given his early history. George Orson Welles first made his presence known to the world on 6 May 1915 in Kenosha, Wisconsin. Father Richard was an inventor, engineer and businessman who owned factories and hotels. Mother Beatrice Ives was from a well-to-do family in the coal business. She was a highly skilled concert pianist, although she did not perform professionally. She knew everybody and it was not uncommon for the intelligentsia to decorate her salon. For the first two years of his life, Orson – he hated to be called George –

could hear the agonising screams of his grandmother, Lucy Ives, who was dying of stomach cancer.

Richard and Beatrice lived different and separate lives so Orson found himself travelling between them. With his father, Orson learned to enjoy life to the full. With his mother (and her gold-digging companion Dr Bernstein), he learned to enjoy art and the finer things in life. Richard and Beatrice officially separated when Orson was six.

On his ninth birthday, Welles visited his mother's room while she was ill with hepatitis – it was the last time he saw her alive. It is not difficult to see the death of Isabel Minafer, handled so sensitively in *The Magnificent Ambersons*, as an echo of this moment.

For short holidays away from school, Orson spent his time with Dr Bernstein. Longer ones were spent travelling the world with his drunkard father – Jamaica, Hong Kong, Shanghai, Beijing. Richard (allegedly) committed suicide three days after Christmas in 1930 and Dr Bernstein became Orson's guardian. There was a trust fund – Orson got a yearly income, and the balance when he was 25. This echoes the trust fund allotted to Charles Foster Kane, who also had a drunkard father.

Much of Welles' work is informed by his politics, which were left wing, like the views formed by many artists in the 1930s.

His first collaboration with producer John Houseman was a play called *Panic!* by Archibald MacLeish, which premiered on 15 March 1935. Welles played McGafferty, a powerful financier. Based on a true story, it tells how McGafferty tries to persuade his colleagues to pool their resources to prevent the panic of 1933. His confidence shattered by the death of his assistant, McGafferty kills himself. *Doctor Faustus* was another play about power. After eventually staging the politically dangerous *The Cradle Will Rock*, the then-theatreless Welles and Houseman set up the Mercury Theatre. Their first production was a modern-dress *Julius Caesar*, with Caesar presented as a fascist, à la Mussolini. It was a critical and commercial success. Welles was pronounced the most innovative stage director in America.

By the early 1940s, Welles was politically active. He supported Franklin D Roosevelt on his presidential campaign and wrote a political column that was syndicated to newspapers nationwide. Welles wanted to run for office in Hollywood but he did not think he had a chance because he was divorced and an actor. He then thought about running for Senator where he grew up, in Wisconsin, but he was dissuaded. Joseph McCarthy won the seat, and Welles subsequently felt guilty about his decision. In 1947, when he could no longer find work in Hollywood and moved to Europe, Welles' political career was effectively terminated. However, the use and abuse of power continued to be a major subject in his films.

One Man Band

'Every actor in his heart believes everything bad that's printed about him.'

Not only did Welles act in and direct films, he also wrote, rewrote, edited and designed most of them. What is more, it was not unknown for him to dub some of the other actors in his films.

Welles got the acting bug early. On 10 July 1918, aged three, he appeared on the stage for his first professional engagement in *Madame Butterfly* as performed by the Chicago Opera Company.

When he had learned the ropes, Welles settled into his niche as a King actor. That is, he could only play one part, the big man in authority, and was particularly adept at showing the fragility of such a man.

Apart from a few notable exceptions (*The Third Man, Jane Eyre, Compulsion*), Welles was rarely offered any big or great parts. He wanted Don Corleone in *The Godfather*, but that was not to be. He accepted parts to live and to pay off his enormous tax bills. He was totally pragmatic about the situation: 'They hire me to add a bit of class.' Welles saw his voice and acting skills as saleable commodities, as tools that allowed him to accumulate money for his own personal projects.

Welles did not use the Method, or create an iconic persona. He liked to literally sculpt the characters he played, using their appearance as a pointer to their motives and emotions. He did not believe the style of the acting mattered. His favourite actor was James Cagney – he was in no way a natural actor, yet he communicated a 'truth' to the audience and they responded to it.

When acting for other directors Welles supplied suggestions for his own dialogue, and sometimes even lighting and camera directions. Over the years, many people have claimed that Welles directed his own sequences as Harry Lime in *The Third Man*, and that the whole film had a certain Wellesian touch. Welles said that director Carol Reed wanted suggestions and he supplied them for his own dialogue. Reed liked the dialogue, so it was used. The direction was completely Reed's.

'Criticism is the essence of creation.' –
Orson Welles, aged 10

Welles' skill as a dramatic writer, especially as an adapter of classics, has been overlooked. He took apart the subject matter and plot, then reassembled the classic in his own style and fashion. In doing so, he did not destroy the spirit of the piece but found a new way of portraying that spirit for a modern audience.

As an example, take his staging of *Moby Dick*. The problem is this: you have some very dense text written by Herman Melville and you have to show ships, water and whales. What does Welles do? Somewhere in his mind he drew a parallel between Ahab's quest for Moby Dick and King Lear's quest for knowledge, then he made this parallel obvious by having a group of actors on stage rehearsing *King Lear*, and an announcement coming that they have to play *Moby Dick* instead. Thus, he uses the play within a play idea (a Shakespearean trait as well as a Wellesian one), and the rehearsal props stand in for the real thing. Therefore, the form of Welles' play becomes as allegorical as the subject of the text. Form and content are melded into one.

Welles' influence on popularising Shakespeare in America cannot be overemphasised. As a child, his mother read Shakespeare to him, which ignited a lifelong passion for the bard. She gave him his first book, *A Midsummer Night's Dream*, for his third birthday. By the age of seven, Orson had memorised all the major speeches from *King Lear*, his favourite Shakespeare play. In the early 1930s, he began writing prompt books for Shakespeare's plays with Skipper Hill, his former headmaster. These were abridgements with detailed stage directions and thousands of illustrations (by Welles) showing facial expressions and body movements. They included extracts from *Chronicles of England Scotlande and Irelande* by Raphael Holinshed, the historical source book Shakespeare had used. Originally published by the Todd School, they proved so popular with students and actors alike that Harper & Brothers published a collection. It sold over 100,000 copies and helped rejuvenate interest in Shakespeare throughout America. Needless to say, Welles' radical interpretations of the plays on stage and in film have influenced the film versions of Shakespeare that have appeared throughout the 1990s.

'My definition of a film director is the man who presides over accidents, but doesn't make them.'

The director is the person who tells everybody else what to do. Welles started at an early age. Dr Maurice Bernstein gave Orson a puppet theatre when he was three. Orson wrote, designed and produced original plays and presented them to his family. When the puppet theatre became too small for his plans, he put on his lifesize plays in the attic, performing all the parts by throwing his voice. From the age of 11 to 15, whilst at the Todd School in Woodstock,

Illinois, headmaster Roger 'Skipper' Hill became Orson's new mentor and encouraged his participation in the Todd Players, who toured the local area performing Orson's abridged versions of Shakespeare.

When he left school, aged 16, Orson travelled around Ireland painting. After landing in Galway, he toured the country in a donkey and cart, eventually arriving in Dublin. On his first night, he saw Micheál MacLiammóir in Gogol's *The Inspector General* at the Gate Theatre. Orson introduced himself to MacLiammóir and his lover Hilton Edwards, owners of the Gate, said that he was an experienced New York actor (which they did not believe) and had his professional debut on 13 October 1931 as the villainous Duke in *Jew Süss*. Welles learnt his craft under the Irish actor/directors, and they remained lifelong friends.

Welles believed that all stories came out of character. He made sure the actors rehearsed before filming, not a common practice in Hollywood. The actors could develop their characters, as they would during a theatre run, and Welles was always open to suggestions.

Also, Welles did not think that a script was set in stone. Once on the set, or on location, he would hand out scenes he had rewritten overnight. He wanted spontaneity, to capture the moment – if the actors were up or down, he would switch scenes to suit their mood. If the light and shadow were correct, perhaps he would invent a shot that would find its way into the finished film.

This is not to say that Welles' artistic nature did not have its bad side – he was prone to throwing tantrums, mainly due to his impatience. He always made up afterwards.

'Movies aren't just made on the set.'

The way film is cut together in a Welles film is unique. It can be very slow, all done in one take. It can ping-pong between two characters. It can be a cascade of conflicting images. The distinct Welles style that evolved over the years was down to one thing: Welles handled, marked and cut the film himself. In America and Britain, the unions forbade anybody but the editor from touching the film. When he moved to Europe in the late 1940s, Welles found that he could pick the film up, look at it, experiment and there was nobody to stop him. He played with the film endlessly, giving himself a greater understanding of the rhythm of scenes. As an editor he became a great illusionist – on *Othello* one scene contained shots that were filmed years and continents apart.

'I'm a lurid character!'

One of Welles' most interesting skills, often overlooked, was as a raconteur and sometimes ruthless self-promoter. (When Welles became the radio voice of *The Shadow*, the show was a national hit. Fan clubs sprouted overnight and Welles made personal appearances in a large hat, red scarf and black cloak.) It was a skill with which he secured finance for his films on more than one occasion.

As a storyteller, he was misdirecting the listener or viewer, making them believe the impossible, which is why he was so interested in magic tricks, in hoaxers, in forgers. (The young Orson received a magic kit from Dr Bernstein and never stopped practising. In later life he was happy to perform his tricks for anybody who showed an interest.)

Welles' greatest hoax was the mock documentary *The War of the Worlds*, broadcast by the Mercury Theatre on Halloween, 30 October 1938. Writer Howard Koch had taken his cue from the radio broadcast of the burning of the Hindenburg the previous year – the newsman on the scene had cried in anguish as the zeppelin burst into flames. Transferring the action of HG Wells' classic from England to New Jersey, the broadcast was taken for real by about six per cent of the total radio audience. There were riots, panic, looting, mobs and a mass exodus from the New Jersey area. When the broadcast finished, irate callers jammed CBS's phone lines and the CBS executives ordered their security people to lock Welles and his players in a back room overnight. The following morning the whole of America knew the name Orson Welles.

Welles reused the mock documentary idea in *F for Fake* and with the *News on the March* sequence in *Citizen Kane*.

The Dreamer

'When you are down and out something always turns up, and it is usually the noses of your friends.'

Welles was a maverick. Which means that the films he wanted to make were not the films Hollywood producers wanted to make. And when Hollywood rejected Welles, he did not give up making movies but went out and raised the money himself. He was an independent producer/director/writer/actor/set designer/editor.

He was a practical man. He was a poet. So what was there in his make-up that prevented Welles from achieving everything he wanted? What was the spark that made him ignore suggestions to compromise?

At the centre of the labyrinth, embedded in his heart of darkness, was a shining beacon: integrity. We live in a world that generally lacks that centre. Integrity is something that can be bought as easily as a bag of chips. Welles had it but would not let anybody, including himself, buy it. I put forward the notion that his continuing popularity is due to that singular asset.

There is a myth that somehow Welles fell from grace, that he did not fulfil his potential, that he should have gone on to make more and better films after *Citizen Kane*. The fact is, he did go on to make other masterpieces: *The Magnificent Ambersons*, *Othello*, *Touch of Evil*, *The Trial* and *Chimes at Midnight*. Commentators fail to mention this in their rush to write saleable copy for magazines. (As Max Beerbohm put it, 'There is much to be said for failure, it is far more interesting than success.')

Whatever they say about him, Welles lived in the present. Everything about him told you that this moment together, on stage, on the radio, in the cinema, was the important thing. Forget the past. Do not imagine the future. Live in the here and now. Live for, and in, this moment of truth.

This is the reason Welles' films are still as vital and fresh as on the day they were made.

Citizen Kane (1941)

'A labyrinth without a centre.' – Jorge Luis Borges on
Citizen Kane

Director, Producer & Co-Writer: Orson Welles

Cast: Orson Welles (Charles Foster Kane), Dorothy
Comingore (Susan Alexander), Joseph Cotten (Jedediah
Leland/Newsreel Reporter), Agnes Moorehead (Mrs
Kane), Ruth Warrick (Emily Norton), Ray Collins (Boss
James 'Jim' W Gettys), Erskine Sanford (Herbert
Carter/Newsreel Reporter), Everett Sloane (Bernstein),
William Alland (Jerry Thompson/*News on the March*
Narrator), Paul Stewart (Raymond), George Coulouris
(Walter Parks Thatcher), Fortunio Bonanova (Matiste),
Alan Ladd (Reporter smoking pipe), Herman J
Mankiewicz (Newspaperman), Gregg Toland (Interviewer
in Newsreel), 118 mins

Working Titles: *American*; *John Citizen, USA*

Story: A 'No Trespassing' sign. In the isolated, decaying
mansion, an old man lies in bed. He whispers 'Rosebud',

a snow globe falls from his grasp and smashes on the floor. He is dead.

News on the March. Start reel: the dead man is Charles Foster Kane, owner of 37 newspapers plus syndicates and radio stations. His mother inherited a large fortune and put both it and her son in the custody of Walter Parks Thatcher. (Thatcher gives Charles a new sled.) Kane's first marriage was in 1900 to Emily Norton, the President's niece. Kane is seen with communist and fascist leaders from all over the world. In 1916, he is caught in a love nest with Susan Alexander. It ends his political career. He builds the Chicago Opera House for her to sing in, then builds Xanadu for her to live in. (Xanadu is the enormous mansion, with its own swimming pools and zoo.) From 1929 to 1933, his papers begin to close. He becomes an old doddering fool, a clown, a laughing stock. End reel.

The reporters in the projection room talk about Kane. Thompson is assigned to talk to everybody to find out what Rosebud means. 'It'll probably turn out to be a very simple thing,' says one. Thompson goes to Atlantic City to talk to Susan Alexander, now a singer at a club. She will not talk. Next, he visits the Walter Parks Thatcher library and reads a memoir.

Thatcher Memoir: 1871. Thatcher collects the child Kane from his mother and drunken father – the mother is suddenly rich from the Colorado Lode. Charles is to be brought up properly. Charles hits Thatcher with his sled. As they leave, Charles' sled is buried under the snow. Growing up, Kane has the world's sixth largest fortune, which he inherits on his twenty-fifth birthday. Kane looks through his assets. What does he want to do? 'I think it would be fun to run a newspaper.' Taking over the editorship of *The Inquirer*, Kane campaigns against Thatcher and other financiers. Kane: 'If I don't look after the interests of the underprivileged, who will?' By 1929, Kane is bust, loses control, signs everything over to Thatcher. He never made a single investment – always buying things. Kane: 'If I hadn't been very rich, I could have been a really great man.' Thatcher: 'What would you have been?' Kane: 'Everything you hated.'

Thompson visits Kane's business manager, Bernstein, at his office.

Bernstein remembers: Kane moves his bed into the office of *The Inquirer* and turns it into a campaigning scandal sheet. Bernstein and Kane's friend Leland are with him. Kane: 'If the headline is big enough it makes the news big.' Kane prints a Declaration of Principles in which he says he will tell the news honestly, tell the truth and champion the people's rights as citizens and humans. Leland keeps the piece of paper on which Kane wrote the principles. Circulation is 26,000. Their competitor, *The Chronicle*, has a circulation of 495,000. Six years later, Kane buys *The Chronicle* and has a circulation of 684,000. Kane celebrates with a big party – dancing girls sing a song about Charlie. Leland is worried that *The Chronicle* men are the right sort of people for the paper – if Kane does not change them, perhaps they will change Kane. Kane goes off to Europe and comes back with Emily Norton.

And what does Bernstein think Rosebud is? Something he wanted, something he lost, something he never had.

Memory is a funny thing. Bernstein remembers one time when he was young he saw a girl in a white dress. There is not a day that goes by when he does not think of her. Bernstein says old age is 'the only disease you never look forward to getting cured of'.

Next is a nursing home, and Jedediah Leland, Kane's best friend, until they had a disagreement.

Jedediah thinks back: over the years Kane and Emily grow apart. Kane becomes more belligerent. Emily does not like Kane attacking the president (her uncle). What will people think? 'What I tell them to think!' says Kane. (Leland: 'Charles wanted love.') Kane is splashed by a passing car and a young woman laughs at him. Susan has a toothache, so he goes back to her room, makes funny noises and faces, and she laughs all night. Kane was on his way to the warehouse in search of his past. Susan wants to sing and Kane makes her sing. Cut to clapping hands – Kane making a political speech, campaigning for office. He promises to smash Boss Jim W Gettys and to do everything in his power to 'protect the underprivileged, underpowered and underfed'. Afterwards, Emily takes him to Susan's room. Gettys is there and says he will give the story of the love nest to the papers unless Kane drops out of the campaign. Kane refuses, the story is headline news and he loses the election. A drunk Leland, disappointed with Kane, tells Kane, 'You talk about the people as though you own them,' and says the working man expects his rights as rights rather than as gifts from Kane. Leland goes to work in Chicago. After Emily and their son die in a car crash, Kane marries Susan and builds an opera house for her. She is not good enough. Afterwards, Kane is at the

Chicago Inquirer. There is only one more review to be handed in – the dramatic notice by Jedediah, who is drunk and asleep on his typewriter. He had started his review, saying Susan stinks. Kane finishes it as it started. They never saw each other again.

Thompson goes back to get Susan Alexander's story. She is drunk at the club where she sings.

Susan's story: she remembers Kane forcing her to have the singing lessons, and the terrible premiere. Kane sees people sleeping and laughing during the performance. When it finishes and the clapping stops, Kane claps on his own, trying to force everybody else to start. After the bad review, Kane sends Leland a big cheque as severance pay – Leland returns it in shreds and with it the Declaration of Principles torn into pieces. Kane stands over Susan to force her to sing – she tries to commit suicide. He sits by her bedside day and night. Susan: 'You don't know what it feels like when the whole audience doesn't want you.' Kane: 'That's when you have to fight them.' Kane stays away from the outside world, keeping Susan and himself locked away in the giant Xanadu mansion. Susan spends her time piecing together jigsaw puzzles. They are a long way apart. Kane brings her on a picnic. We hear the song 'It Can't Be Love' in the background. Susan and Kane argue. Susan: 'You keep trying to bribe me into giving you something', 'You don't love me. You don't even love you!' Kane slaps her. Susan leaves Xanadu. Kane is afraid of what people might think.

Thompson is at Xanadu, talks to Raymond, the butler. What about Rosebud?

Raymond remembers: when Susan left, Kane broke up

the room, then picked up a snow globe and whispered 'Rosebud'. Walking down a corridor, we see many Kanes reflected in the mirror.

Thompson and his photographers walk through the accumulated statues and objects discussing what Rosebud might be. Something he couldn't get or lost? Playing with one of Susan's jigsaws, Thompson says that Rosebud is the missing piece of the puzzle, which would help us see the whole picture. The reporters leave and we float over a sea of objects filling the mansion. We stop over an old sled. It is picked up and thrown in a furnace. It is called Rosebud. Smoke floats up from the furnace. We see the 'No Trespassing' sign of Xanadu.

Visual Ideas: Cinematographer Gregg Toland had photographed a snow globe in *Kitty Foyle* a few years earlier. An influence? Certainly.

Tracking Shots Aplenty: going in through the roof of the club where Susan Alexander performs; down from the statue in the Thatcher library; up from the opera stage to the men in the rigging above.

Lighting: the ray of light shining down from above, illuminating the Thatcher memoirs; the up-lighting on the dancers in the newspaper office making it look like the limelight of a stage show.

Transitions: from a photo of *The Chronicle* staff, a light flash, and it is the same people lined up for a photo for *The Inquirer*; when Susan sings for Kane to the clapping hands at Kane's speech.

Brilliance: the breakfast scene spinning back and forth between Kane and Emily. Each shot is later in time.

Through this we see both the deterioration of the relationship and Kane's evolution from fun-loving newsman to corrupt dictator.

Visual Symbolism: we see Kane through lots of different pieces of film (the newsreel) and through the eyes of the people who were around him. At the end, when Kane walks past the mirror, we see this represented visually (one man can be seen from many different angles, each one a distortion, but none of them is the real thing). The idea of different pieces of Kane being put together to make the whole picture is explicitly compared to a jigsaw when Thompson holds Susan's jigsaw pieces.

Audio Ideas: From the whisper of 'Rosebud' we go to the loud newsreel. The loud noise idea is repeated elsewhere: when we go to a close-up of Kane's hands typing Jedediah's bad review; also the parakeet squawking when Kane breaks up Susan's room.

Themes: Starts with a death. The mystery is 'Who or what is Rosebud?' The fall of the big man. Finding out the truth through interviews. The screen is represented by the *News on the March* sequence and the opera stage. The fragility of power. The abuse of power. Corrupt authority. Man caught in a web. Betrayal. Clinging to innocence. Servile acceptance. Self-destruction. Power corrupts. Jedediah clings to integrity whilst Kane loses it.

Subtext: Kane wanted people to love him, so the rise in newspaper circulation meant that more people loved him. He was serving the people. He believed that he knew better than the people, and could help them better themselves. He corrupted this idea into, 'I know better so people must do what I say.' He became a bully. This is symbolised by his acquisition of Susan, whom he 'improves' by bullying her into being a singer. When she leaves, there is a limp doll in the foreground of the picture – meaning she is no longer a child and will not be treated as Kane's plaything anymore. The doll image is important – from the time of his trip to Europe, Kane acquired statues (he does not know why he buys them) and his first wife. The statues are people he has bought who can never leave him.

Money: this film suggests that money is unimportant and bad. Kane spends it all, to be rid of it. He figuratively and literally buys people with it.

That Darned Sled: when Thatcher takes Charles away from his mother, we see the sled being buried under snow. In the newsreel, we see Thatcher giving Charles a new sled, which he does not like. The snow globe and the sled represent both his innocence (before he had money), and the last time he was loved for himself and not for his money. Charles wants love not money – this is shown symbolically when he hits Thatcher with the sled.

Background: After the Halloween 1938 broadcast of *The War of the Worlds*, the whole of America knew the name Orson Welles. He was hot property. Consequently, RKO offered Welles lots of money to direct a film. He did not want to make movies, so RKO kept offering him more money because they wanted a prestige name to bolster the studio. Then, when they could not offer more money, they said Welles could write, direct, star and have complete artistic control, but he had to deliver his film under a set budget. Welles agreed and RKO publicised the agreement. It is not surprising that a lot of Hollywood resented the power and the deal he had secured. It was very rare for actors to direct themselves. George Shaefer, the head of RKO at the time, took a big risk with Welles, and was confident in Welles' ability to make art and money at the same time.

Myth: Welles had not directed a film before *Citizen Kane*. Truth: he made a 40-minute short called *Too Much Johnson* in 1938, starring Joseph Cotten. It was made to accompany a production of WS Gillette's play. There was a 20-minute prologue to Act One, plus 10-minute introductions to Acts Two and Three. George Shaefer saw this slapstick comedy footage before offering Welles a contract. Also, in the summer of 1934, Welles and Skipper Hill organised the Woodstock Drama Festival at Todd. It was there that Welles made his first film, *Hearts of Age*, a 10-minute home movie shot in an afternoon.

Myth: Welles had complete freedom on his RKO contract. Truth: Welles signed a two-picture deal on 22 July 1939, which gave him the freedom to submit three ideas for each film, which RKO could object to. RKO would then submit their three ideas.

Myth: Welles had complete power. Truth: nobody could be hired by Welles, not even his Mercury people, without RKO's approval. Welles was to show the rushes to the studio people and to confer with them about the final cut. RKO could alter the film in any way they chose for censorship reasons and for foreign markets.

In summary, Welles had a great contract but not the carte blanche contract that people thought he had, and which gained him so much enmity within the Hollywood community.

July 1939, Welles arrived in Hollywood and filled his offices with 22/23-year-old kids – they were in stark contrast to the old guard at RKO. Work began on *Heart of Darkness*, an adaptation of the Joseph Conrad novella. The camera would be the narrator Marlow, and Kurtz would be both victim and perpetrator of the modern totalitarian state. It was shelved because Welles could not get the budget he needed. Shaefer had great confidence in Welles and gave him his head in all areas except budget. Then Welles began work on the Hitchcockian comedy/thriller *Smiler With a Knife*, based on British fascist Sir Oswald Mosley, but that was stopped because of the political overtones.

Welles' last choice was *American*, the story of a big man who falls, as seen from various people's point of view. The idea came from Herman J Mankiewicz, a burnt-out, drunken screenwriter, known for his witty one-liners, who needed to make a comeback. First it was to be based on Howard Hughes, as played by Joseph Cotten, and be an attack on the acquisitive society. Then the plot was changed so it became about a man who, foolishly, marries a woman and builds her an opera house so that she can sing. This is a direct lift of the life of Samuel Insull, who built the Chicago Opera House for his wife Gladys Wallace. The incident of a drunk Jedediah starting to write a bad review then sleeping on the typewriter really happened to Mankiewicz when reviewing Miss Wallace.

Mankiewicz had once been a regular at William Randolph Hearst's San Simeon. No longer welcome at the home of Hearst and his mistress Marion Davies, Mankiewicz was happy to use his insider knowledge to add a bit of vitriol to the script. Welles and Mankiewicz had found their subject.

There has been major controversy about who wrote *Citizen Kane*. First, let me say that Frank Brady's book *Citizen Welles* puts everything in perspective because he has read every piece of paper pertaining to the question. It happened like this. Beginning May 1940, for 12 weeks, Mankiewicz wrote a 250-page script, based on Welles' ideas, whilst being supervised and edited by John Houseman. (In fact, Mankiewicz had broken his leg, so he dictated his notes, and Houseman was also there to ensure Mankiewicz stayed away from the booze.) After six weeks, Welles saw the first 100 pages. He okayed, rewrote or binned pages. Welles took out all the very specific material about Hearst (especially the libellous stuff), slimmed it down considerably, added episodes from his own life and made it more intimate. In other words, he rewrote the text and made it come alive for him, as he had done for countless other projects. This process continued for five drafts until the script was written.

A lot remains close to Hearst's life. Bernstein (from Dr Bernstein) is based on Hearst's business manager SS Carvalho. Jedediah Leland is Chicago newspaper columnist Ashton Stevens. Jim W Gettys is Boss Charles W Murphy, who campaigned against Hearst in New York. Walter P Thatcher is financier JP Morgan. Kane's line, 'Dear Wheeler, you provide the prose poems, I'll provide the war,' was a direct steal from Hearst's reply to artist Frederic Remington who was covering the Spanish-American War in 1896. The Declaration of Principles was also Hearst's. The circulation figures for Kane's *Inquirer* were the same as those for Hearst's *Examiner*. Xanadu was obviously San Simeon. Although Hearst did not buy an opera house for Marion Davies, he did buy a film studio, Cosmopolitan Pictures, so she could be a movie star. If Welles is to be believed, Rosebud was Hearst's pet name for Marion Davies' private parts. The list goes on. There are so many parallels to Hearst's life in the dialogue and details that in retrospect it really is a miracle that they got away with it. Today, they would all be in court and penniless.

Arguments arose because Welles wanted to pay Mankiewicz not to take any credit for the script; his contract with RKO said that he must have sole writing credit. In the end both Mankiewicz and Welles are credited as writers on the final film, which is as it should be.

Scenes which were scripted and storyboarded but never made it into the final film include: Kane's honeymoon; Kane's son Howard growing up to become a fascist, getting killed and being buried in Xanadu; Susan's lover being killed by Kane (the alleged story behind the suspicious death of Thomas H Ince was that Hearst killed him because he was sleeping with Marion Davies); a brothel scene after the celebration at *The Inquirer*.

Welles had this great new toy, but did not know how to use it yet, so decided to test it out. He shot tests for ten days, starting 29 June 1940, beginning with the projection-room scene. (It was normal procedure for films to start with tests and use the footage later.) The cast was important to Welles. They were his Mercury Theatre players, who had worked with him both on radio and in the theatre, and all but one were new to cinema. The interviews with the different characters were done on existing sets of current productions. Actors were pushed to their limits, told to reshoot and reshoot – Joseph Cotten, playing Leland near death, had to repeat his lines 108 times! For his drunk scene, Cotten was kept awake and filming for 24 hours to get the right worn-out feeling. None of this could have been done without the aid of Gregg Toland, the crew and all the other technicians and craftsmen who rallied around Welles.

Welles finished filming 11 days over his 15-week schedule, and barely over budget, then gave all the film to Robert Wise to edit. Wise put together the *News on the March* newsreel himself, degrading some of the film by dragging it across the cement floor of the editing room.

When word got out to Hearst that *Citizen Kane* was about him, he banned all mention of it in his 30 major newspapers nationwide. The film was sent to RKO's New York office to see whether or not it could be released. Many of the cinema chains refused to take it. For a time there was a possibility that all prints of the film would be burnt.

On opening night in San Francisco, Welles stepped into his hotel elevator and found Hearst already in there. Welles offered Hearst tickets to the premiere, but Hearst did not reply. (Welles later said that Kane would have taken the tickets. To me, this sounds like a story Welles concocted for the biographers.) There were dirty tricks as well. One night, Welles was called aside by a cop who said that Welles should not go back to his hotel that night – there was a naked underage girl in his room, and some photographers waiting to snap him with her.

It has never been made clear why Welles chose to attack Hearst through *Citizen Kane*. If it was purely political then Hearst was a prime target – he was a right-winger, controlled much of America's media, advocated that America keep out of World War Two, supported Hitler and even went so far as to fake an interview with Hitler which was to reassure the West of his intentions. All these activities greatly angered people on the left, which included Welles' friends.

At the premiere in May 1941, *Citizen Kane* was a complete critical success – they went wild over it – but it did not do great business. It was hurt by the lack of publicity, and those who did go were confused by many of the innovations contained therein. At the time, it was probably the world's most expensive art film. Since then, it has often been quoted as the best American film ever made.

The Verdict: A vibrant, entrancing film that pulses with energy. I love it. 5/5

The Magnificent Ambersons (1942)

'A film is never really good unless the camera is an eye
in the head of a poet.'

Director & Writer: Orson Welles

Cast: Joseph Cotten (Eugene Morgan), Dolores Costello
(Isabel Amberson Minafer), Anne Baxter (Lucy Morgan),
Tim Holt (George Amberson Minafer), Agnes Moorehead
(Fanny Minafer), Ray Collins (Jack Amberson), Erskine
Sanford (Roger Bronson), Richard Bennett (Major
Amberson), Orson Welles (Narrator), 88 mins

Story: In 1873, the pace of life was slow. Everybody
knew everybody else's horse and carriage, and the
streetcar would stop and wait for you. But times were
changing, as were the fashions. The Ambersons, the main
family in town, had even installed bathrooms and water
closets into the bedrooms. Young Eugene Morgan spent
his time courting the affections of Isabel Amberson. But
he made a fool of himself one night, when trying to sere-
nade her, by falling through a bass fiddle – he was drunk
– and that was the end of that. Well, Isabel married boring,
dependable Wilbur Minafer and had a child with him,

Georgie. Since she did not love Wilbur, she poured all her love into Georgie. This was reciprocated – the spoiled brat got into fights defending her. Folks around town hoped they would live to see the day of his comeuppance.

Twenty years later, the town sees its last great dance, hosted by the Ambersons. Widower Eugene Morgan arrives back in town and when Isabel sees him it is obvious they are still in love. Eugene and Isabel dance into the night, oblivious to the others around them. George takes an instant dislike to Eugene and tells his new beautiful companion so. Lucy says that she is Eugene's daughter.

Of course, George courts Lucy, and during winter takes her out in a horse-drawn sled, while Eugene takes the rest of the family out in a horseless carriage. George and Lucy crash (literally falling for each other) and are rescued by the automobile.

Aunt Fanny sets her cap for Eugene – Uncle Jack and George see this chink in her formidable armour and tease her, making her cry. No matter how much Fanny loves him, Eugene only has eyes for Isabel.

Wilbur dies – he became ill after making some unwise investments.

George wants to marry Lucy but she refuses because he has no way of supporting her. Reacting to his rejection, when the subject of cars is raised over dinner and the consensus is that cars are changing the face of the land, George says they are a nuisance. Eugene is thoughtful and comments that technology alters both war and peace. 'Perhaps automobiles had no business to be invented,' he says and then leaves.

Fanny, lashing out because she too is rejected, tells George that everybody in town is talking about Isabel and Eugene and saying that they were together before Wilbur died. George goes wild, questioning people, telling them to stop gossiping about his mother.

When Eugene comes to take Isabel out, George sends him away. Unaware of this, Isabel dutifully waits to be taken out. Then Eugene sends a letter to Isabel, saying that she must choose between George and himself. He pleads, 'Please don't strike my life down twice.' Isabel and George decide to leave indefinitely, to go to Europe. Eugene says he will wait.

Meeting Lucy on the street, George says this is the last time they will meet... ever. Lucy is cheerful and makes fun of it. When George leaves, she faints.

Time passes. Isabel becomes ill in Paris and George will not let her go home. Then Isabel returns home in a horse and carriage. When Eugene comes to visit, he cannot see her because she is too ill. She dies, as does her father Major Amberson, soon afterwards.

With no money, the house is sold to pay off debts, and George looks for employment so that he can support Aunt Fanny. Then George is run down by a car and both his legs are broken. Eugene visits him and decides to help him, saying that he must because he is Isabel's son. He feels that, at last, 'I've been true to my true love.'

Visual Ideas: This film is so visually rich it would take a book just to explain it. There are some outstanding images: the constant use of silhouette on Isabel gives her a timeless, classical quality; the camera prowling through the house during the dance; characters all different sizes, separated and seemingly floating in black space; the camera following Fanny and George up the stairs as Fanny spills the beans on Isabel and Eugene; the shot looking up to three levels of the staircase, with a character on each level; the prowling camera showing the grimy houses as George makes his (literally) last walk to the Amberson mansion.

Audio Ideas: When Major Amberson is looking into the fire at the end, mumbling, his speech becomes progressively dimmer. The image and sound are so poignant, it brings a lump to my throat. I feel as though I am looking into Richard Bennett's essence.

This is a very loud picture with music and machinery, overlapping dialogue and voiceovers driving it. The only time it is quiet is when somebody dies. It even goes quiet when the house dies.

Themes: Fall of the family. George's self-destruction. The fragility of power when you have no money. Isabel's servile acceptance of George's wishes.

Subtext: This is an elegy for the old America, explained through a family destroyed by cars. Like Falstaff in *Chimes at Midnight*, the family does not move with the times and so is ruined. This is explained through George Minafer, who has the love of his mother and will do everything in his power to prevent her giving any of it away to Eugene Morgan. This love for his mother even overshadows his love for Lucy. George is jealous of Eugene, hence his hatred for the inventor, technology and the modern age. From the start, everybody in town cannot wait for the day when Georgie Minafer gets his comeuppance. It comes, in spades, with the death of his mother, the loss of Lucy and, ironically, both his legs are broken in an auto accident.

The Magnificent Ambersons shows America's changing attitude to money. At the beginning, one did not talk of money – it was a vulgar subject. Even when Wilbur makes a few wrong investments, it does not concern others in the house – they are ladies and gentlemen and have no need of a profession. This is contrasted with the rise of the Morgans, who are practical people. The only time they talk of money is obtusely in the song 'The Man Who Broke the Bank at Monte Carlo' – money as a plaything. When Isabel and Major Amberson are dead and all the money is gone, at the train station Uncle Jack refers to himself and George as 'two gentlemen of elegant appearance in a state of busti-tude'. Finally, George and Aunt Fanny talk about the amount of dollars they need to live. 'You certainly are the most practical man I ever met,' she tells him. At last, George is taking responsibility for what remains of the Ambersons. He even goes so far as to go to a law office, get a job and talk about the amount of money he would receive – a conversation he could never previously contemplate.

Background: For his second film, Welles wanted to get away from the controversy of Citizen Kane and give RKO a film they wanted. The Magnificent Ambersons had it all: a family saga; a turn-of-the-century setting; a bittersweet love story; young lovers and unrequited love; the loss of a fortune; a riches-to-rags story.

Welles was very familiar with the subject. He first adapted the fall of the Ambersons when the Mercury Theatre broadcast a radio show on 29 October 1939. Walter Huston played Eugene Morgan, whilst Welles played the spoilt George Minafer. To fit the hour-long format, Welles had completely cut Aunt Fanny and Wilbur Minafer from the story, but the ending was the same as in Booth Tarkington's novel. Welles later claimed the character of Eugene Morgan had been based on Welles' father – it is certainly possible since Richard Welles and Booth Tarkington had known each other. Richard even owned Badger Brass, manufacturer of one of the earliest automobile lights.

To persuade the bosses at RKO that this was a suitable film project, Welles played a recording of the radio show, and they were all convinced. RKO were even more encouraged because they acquired the rights for a song – Warner Brothers bought the rights in 1929, had two unfilmable scripts written and were happy to unload it. Welles stowed himself away on director King Vidor's yacht and wrote the first draft screenplay in nine days.

Because of a dwindling world market – there was a war in Europe, after all – RKO had set a maximum budget of $600,000 in Welles' contract. (RKO had agreed with their bank that they would not finance films with a budget over $750,000.) But the initial estimates for *The Magnificent Ambersons* came in at over $1 million. They were pared down to $850,000, and Welles gave his assurances that he would do everything in his power to keep costs down. George Shaefer, head of RKO, gave the okay.

Film actors usually perform little bits at a time and film

their scenes out of sequence. This means they have little or no opportunity to develop, grow and refine their characters as they would on a run in the theatre. Welles, coming from a theatre background, decided to rehearse his actors for six weeks. The actors were allowed to make appropriate changes to the script during that time.

The outdoor snow scenes were shot in a Los Angeles ice house so that as the actors spoke you could see the fog on their breath – Ray Collins contracted pneumonia. For the sled crash, Welles made Tim Holt and Anne Baxter perform the stunt because he wanted close-ups of their faces.

For one scene, the camera was strapped to a camera operator, who walked through six empty rooms, walls and ceiling flying apart behind him to allow the necessary camera equipment to be moved with him. Despite the hard work, the shot was not in the final cut.

With filming complete, the editing began. However, Welles was already working on *Journey Into Fear* – he had designed the storyboards and filmed his own scenes (as Colonel Haki) in the evenings after working all day on *The Magnificent Ambersons*. Then on 4 February 1942, Welles went to Rio de Janeiro to film *It's All True*, a documentary supported by the US Government as part of the war propaganda effort. Welles left *Journey Into Fear* to Norman Foster to direct and *The Magnificent Ambersons* to Robert Wise to edit.

Some scenes had to be refilmed by Wise, Jack Moss (magician and Welles' business manager), Freddie Fleck and Vernon Walker (special-effects man). When RKO did a preview showing of the two-hour final cut, the viewers' comments were disastrous. According to Wise, people laughed at the performances. (In later years, a further look at the preview cards showed that for everyone that said it was bad, there was another who said it was the greatest film ever made.) Schaefer was distraught because the film had cost over $1 million and RKO needed to make their money back as soon as possible.

Welles sent several lists of edits but they were not carried out. Schaefer, Cotten, Moss and Wise talked about what to do. Schaefer wrote to Welles saying that *Citizen Kane* was never going to make money and *The Magnificent Ambersons* was going the same way. He appreciated that Welles had brought great prestige to RKO but he would ruin the company if his film did not make money. RKO decided to do two things. First they would write and film three additional scenes to add clarity. This included making the ending more upbeat. RKO also decided to bring the running time down to 90 minutes.

The film was recut, 45 minutes disappeared, and the last three scenes were neither written nor directed by Welles. The major problem, as far as Welles was concerned, was that it had an upbeat ending. The Ambersons were too magnificent when they should have been dragged through the gutter and made to smell their own fear and failure.

The Magnificent Ambersons was released in mid-August 1942, when nobody in their right mind would be in a non-air-conditioned room when they could be sunning themselves on vacation. Some critics called it a master-piece, which was reflected in its four Oscar nominations. Most called it a disaster, and it lost over $600,000, an enor-mous sum at that time. Schaefer lost his job.

Although Hollywood did not want Welles the director, they still desired Welles the actor. For the rest of his life, Welles could not fail to make money from his acting. His directing career was another story.

The Verdict: This is magnificent from beginning to end. The subject, the photography, the acting are so bleak and complex even David Lynch would have trouble trying to make it darker. It hurts to think that there was a two-hour version at the preview that is forever denied us. 5/5

The Stranger (1946)

'Your job is to make money.'

Director: Orson Welles

Cast: Orson Welles (Charles Rankin/Franz Kindler),
Edward G Robinson (Wilson), Loretta Young (Mary
Longstreet Rankin), Philip Merivale (Judge Longstreet),
Richard Long (Noah Longstreet), Konstantin Shayne
(Konrad Meinike), Billy House (Mr Potter), 95 mins

Story: An unseen man with a pipe in the Allied War
Crimes Commission wants to let one of his prisoners run
so that they can catch a bigger fish.

A nervous man on a steamboat makes his way across
the world to find Charles Rankin in Harper, Connecticut,
at the heart of small-town America. He is followed by
the man with the pipe. At a boys' school, the nervous
man (Meinike) knocks out the pipe man with athletic
equipment. Meinike goes to Rankin's house, but Mary
Longstreet is there. Meinike waits. Eventually, he catches
up with Rankin, Professor of English – he used
to be Franz Kindler, mastermind of the Holocaust.
Rankin is getting married that evening, thereby

completing his disguise and integrating into American society.

Some boys, out on a paperchase, tell Rankin that they will catch up with him later. Rankin goes into the woods and meets with Meinike, who has converted to Christianity and wants to pray for Kindler's sins. As they kneel to pray, Kindler strangles the old man. The 'hare' runs past them, leaving a trail of paper behind him. Kindler desperately reroutes the paper. 'This way fellas. Don't let him get away!' the paperchasers shout as they run by.

Rankin gets married, and is watched from across the road by Wilson, the man with the pipe. Wilson talks to wily/sly Mr Potter, a big man who does not move but gets all his customers to serve themselves, whether it be coffee or cough drops. Potter and Wilson play checkers as they try to find out information about each other.

During the wedding celebrations, Rankin goes back to the woods to bury Meinike. While Rankin is away on his honeymoon, Wilson checks all the recent arrivals in Harper. He finds out Rankin likes spending a lot of time up in the town's clock tower, which has not worked in decades. There are no photos or descriptions of Kindler – the only thing Wilson knows is that Kindler's hobby was clocks.

When Rankin returns, Wilson is waiting. Over dinner, Wilson angles the conversation around to Germany. Rankin advocates the destruction of Germany and then says, 'Marx wasn't a German. He was a Jew.'

Taking Mary's dog Red for a walk, Red begins digging up Meinike, so Rankin kicks him. Wilson wakes up and realises that Rankin is Kindler, then enlists Mary's brother Noah to help trap the Nazi. They have to try and convince Mary that she made a mistake, that the wonderful man she married and is in love with is a mass murderer. When Mary begins to suspect (because she had met Meinike), Rankin tells her that that man was blackmailing him.

Red turns up dead; poisoned. Wilson and the rest of Mary's family show Mary footage from the concentration camps and try to persuade her of Rankin's guilt but she refuses to believe. Mary denies she could love such a man. Fraught, she confronts Rankin in the clock tower. Then the chimes ring, at 11pm, for the first time in years. The whole town comes out to see – Rankin and Mary have to put on a face for the crowd.

Wilson says Mary is the bait, and will crack. When that happens, Rankin will try to get rid of her since she is the only one with any evidence against him. They have to watch Mary 24 hours a day.

The strain tells on Mary – she cracks up at a party – and Rankin realises he has to kill her to shut her up. He saws the ladder going up to the clock tower, then arranges for Mary to go up it. Only she does not go and sends Noah instead. Rankin waits at Potter's, establishing an alibi for himself, then returns home. He is shocked to find Mary still alive.

Mary knows that Rankin is Kindler. Kindler makes a run for it. When everybody is out looking, Mary goes to the clock tower and confronts Kindler. Up there, Kindler feels like a god. Looking down, he says, 'Would you really care if one of those ants died?'

Wilson arrives. A shoot-out. Kindler catches a bullet, goes out on the clock face. The chimes set the clock in motion. He is impaled on the sword of one of the clock figures and falls to his death.

Visual Ideas: Signs. As Meinike leaves the gym, after knocking out Wilson, the sign on the door clearly reads 'Anyone using equipment does so at own risk', which echoes ironic signs in other Welles movies. Also, when Kindler rings Mary, he absentmindedly doodles a swastika on the pad, then draws over it. There is some sharp photography from Russell Metty, who has a good eye for detail and composition. Aside from the angles necessitated by working within the tall clock tower, there is very little in the look and feel that suggests Welles was the director. When Mary faints after confronting Kindler, she blurs, just as Vargas would blur many years later in *Touch of Evil*.

Audio Ideas: Kindler's speech at the end, about people as ants, is a precursor of Welles' famous scene as Harry Lime in *The Third Man*, on a Ferris wheel, when Lime refers to people as ants. The chimes always seem to signify that someone has died, just as the bell tolled for people in Welles' film of *Macbeth*.

Themes: Irony: Kindler is killed by his own wife (the person who loves him) and by his own hand (the clock he fixed). The mystery: Wilson is trying to find out the truth, but we know who Kindler is all along, so there is no mystery of suspense. Masks: Kindler and Wilson wear 'masks'. Potter puts on different hats depending on which job he is doing. The screen: the concentration-camp footage. Clinging to innocence: Mary tries desperately to remain ignorant. Corrupt authority: Rankin is in a position of authority and responsibility.

Background: Welles' reputation was so low in Hollywood that he needed a project to show he could direct a standard Hollywood film on time and on budget, just like anyone else. He took on *The Stranger* and made sure there was nothing unusual about the angles he used or the editing technique. It was made for William Goetz of International Pictures, who wanted to begin a long-term relationship with Welles. Goetz promised Welles a four-picture deal if he got the film in on time and on budget.

The producer was Sam Spiegel, a protégé of Harry Cohn, and a man to whom you never said no. Ernest Nims, an executive and editor, cut about 32 pages of Anthony Veiller's script before filming began.

Originally, Welles wanted Agnes Moorehead to play the Nazi-hunter, but Edward G Robinson played the part instead. Edward G sulked because Welles was shooting his bad side, so Loretta Young allowed Welles to shoot her 'bad' side so that tough guy Edward G could look more beautiful.

Billy House, a vaudeville comedian in his first film role, was also annoyed. House said that Welles was torturing him. Had he got the job or not? House thought that his stand-in was also up for the part.

It was a disciplined shoot. Welles completed filming under budget and one day under schedule. Ernest Nims edited the film to the bone. According to Welles, he shot 20 minutes of story set in South America which he thought was the best thing about the film – Nims and Spiegel cut it.

Upon release, *The Stranger* did no business, so Goetz made a choice not to give Welles a four-picture deal. Welles decided to do the only sensible thing – go back to the theatre, produce and finance an enormous show out of his own pocket, and put himself into debt. The name of the show was *Around the World in Eighty Days*.

The Verdict: If you excised all the kinks and oddities usually found in a Welles film, it would still be watchable, but it would be dead. This is a dead film. Its single redeeming feature is Billy House as Potter – a standout performance. The most interesting aspect of this failure is that it proves that Welles could not produce work of merit when he did not have the freedom to create. 2/5

The Lady from Shanghai (1947)

'I have a much poorer opinion of my life's work than
you could possibly guess.'

Director & Writer: Orson Welles

Cast: Rita Hayworth (Elsa Bannister), Orson Welles
(Michael O'Hara), Everett Sloane (Arthur Bannister),
Glenn Anders (George Grisby), Ted de Corsica (Sidney
Broome), Erskine Sanford (Judge), Gus Schilling (Goldie),
87 mins

Story: Night. New York. Central Park. Michael, an
Irishman, is taken by the beauty of a woman in a carriage.
He offers her his last cigarette. She does not smoke, but to
please him she takes it anyway, wraps it in a handkerchief
and puts it in her purse. Walking on, Michael hears a
scream. He runs to the woman and fights off the thugs.
Retrieving her purse, he finds a gun in it. Why did she not
pull a gun on her attackers? Elsa says she does not know
how to fire a gun. She offers Michael a job, but he refuses
because she is married.

The next day Michael is looking for a job on a boat.
Arthur Bannister, an older man, who has to use two sticks

to walk, offers him a job and they get drunk with some of Michael's friends. They figure that a tough guy is a guy with an edge, like a knife or a gun. Bringing Bannister back to his yacht, Michael and his friend Goldie agree to work on board – Bannister is Elsa's husband.

They sail all over the West Indies. Elsa swimming, diving into the sea, sunning herself. Grisby, Bannister's partner, arrives, looks at Elsa with a leer in his eye, then leaves. Elsa comes on to Michael. He slaps her. They kiss. Grisby sees them. Elsa says, 'Now he knows about us.' 'I wish I knew,' Michael replies.

They all go on a picnic into a dangerous jungle. Bannister says there is a plot against his life. Elsa says that if she divorced she would not get a cent. (She cannot leave Bannister because he knows of her seedy past in Shanghai and Macao.) Grisby just leers. Arguing among themselves, Elsa asks why anyone would want to be around them. Michael tells them of one time he was fishing and hooked a shark. The shark got free, but the blood from the wound attracted other sharks – soon the sea was full of them, whipped into a frenzy, eating each other alive.

Grisby asks Michael if he would kill somebody for $5,000. 'I'm particular about who I murder,' he answers. When it becomes clear to Michael that the only way he can have Elsa is to have some money, he asks Grisby who he has to murder? 'Me!' Grisby tells Michael. Grisby wants to disappear, get away from his wife, from the firm. The only way he can do it is if Michael signs a confession saying that he killed Grisby, then Grisby could disappear without anybody looking for him, and Michael would be free because, in California, if there is no body, there is no murder.

They land in San Francisco, at each other's throats. Secretly meeting Elsa at an aquarium, Michael tells her everything, that it is the only way they can be together.

The night of the 'murder'. Broome, Bannister's butler, knows what is going on so Grisby shoots him. Grisby then drives with Michael to the scene of the 'murder'. They smash into the back of a truck. Grisby says the truck driver will make a good witness. At the Bannister house, Broome tells Elsa that Grisby shot him. At the harbour, Grisby disappears in a boat and Michael shoots. There are witnesses who see him with a smoking gun. Then it dawns on Michael – Grisby is going to shoot Bannister! The police surround Bannister's office. Grisby is dead. The police stop Michael, take the gun from him, and read his confession. The wrong man is dead and the wrong man is arrested.

Arthur Bannister, the great criminal lawyer who has never lost a case, decides to defend Michael for both murders: Grisby and Broome. The trial is not about a man fighting for his life but a show with the judge, District Attorney and Bannister as the entertainers. The DA calls Bannister as a witness and then Bannister makes a mockery of the process by cross-examining himself. Elsa attends court and looks adoringly at Michael. She has even learned to smoke since she first met him. When she is called as a witness, her love for Michael is made public.

When the jury are on their way back, Bannister tells Michael that he will be going to the Death House every day to gloat, and that he hopes Michael lives for as long as possible so that the agony can be prolonged. Michael swallows Bannister's painkiller pills, overdosing, and all pandemonium breaks loose.

In the judge's office, they desperately try to revive Michael. One by one they leave until Michael is alone with a single guard, who he overpowers. He gets out of the building as a member of another jury, and makes his way through Chinatown. Elsa, seeing him run, follows. Using her knowledge of the Chinese language, she hunts him down to a Chinese theatre. Sitting together, trying to escape from the police, they embrace. Michael is feeling the effect of the pills he took. He takes Elsa's gun and puts it into her ribs. He has worked it out – Elsa is the killer. She killed Grisby. He passes out.

Michael wakes in a funfair crazy house. Everything is clear to him now: Elsa and Grisby planned to kill Bannister using Michael as an alibi, but when Grisby killed Broome she knew they could not get away with it, so she warned Bannister. Michael was the fall guy.

Michael falls through the floor, into a hall of mirrors. Elsa has a gun. Bannister appears with his own gun. They are all reflected with many images. You do not know which is the real them and which is the fake. 'Killing you is killing myself,' Bannister says. He has left a letter with the DA. If he dies, the DA will learn all about Elsa. They shoot. All the mirrors are shattered. Bannister is shot dead. Elsa lies on the floor, dying. 'Don't leave me!' she shouts to Michael. Michael walks away and leaves the sharks behind.

Visual Ideas: There is a surreal meeting between Michael and Elsa at an aquarium with giant turtles swimming in the background. The other excellent surreal scene is the shoot-out in the funhouse hall of mirrors.

Audio Ideas: The voiceover of the main character, which became such a fad after *Murder My Sweet/Farewell, My Lovely* was released, is satirised here. Michael's voice-over as the hero is unheroic and ironic. He is also quite stupid.

When Elsa says she does not know how to fire a gun, Michael tells her it is easy, you just point the gun and pull the trigger. This echoes Lauren Bacall's advice to Humphrey Bogart about whistling in *To Have and Have Not* – 'You just put your lips together and blow.'

The trial scene is played for laughs and all solemnity and tension are continually undermined by sneezing, coughing and other such interruptions by the jury and gallery. Some of the dialogue cannot be heard.

Themes: Finding the truth. The mystery in this movie is not 'Why does Elsa love Michael?', 'Why does Grisby want to be dead?' or 'Why does Elsa stay with Bannister?' It is, 'Why does Michael not ask these questions?' This is a mystery story where the central character is too dumb to ask questions. Masks: everybody is pretending to be something they are not. The screen: this is about the way stories, and films in particular, are told. When we first see Elsa in the park, the flickering light on her face makes it look like a silent movie. Just as the hall-of-mirrors sequence at the end looks like a strip of Edward Muybridge's photos from the late 1800s. This disjointed approach to images is apparent in the scene where Elsa sings on the boat. Each of the main characters is shown apart, so that you do not know their relationship to each other – which is the central mystery of the film. Elsa and Michael talk in front of the aquarium windows, which look like film screens. Loss of integrity, betrayal, abuse of power, man caught in a web and clinging to integrity also feature as important themes.

Subtext: The story is about a sea full of sharks acquiring a bloodlust and eating each other alive. Michael is a not-so-innocent man used as bait by each of the other sharks. He is stupid, but he is not evil.

There is a Chinese saying that if someone follows their nature, they follow their original nature to the end of their days. In the funhouse, Michael asks Elsa why she could not find something better to follow. At one stage, Elsa says that everything is bad, that you cannot run away from it, that you have to make a deal with it to survive. The extension to this is that, when you deal with bad things, a part of you becomes bad. You are corrupted. The question at the end of the movie is: will Michael be corrupted by this experience? His answer is that he will try to forget Elsa. Maybe he will die trying. Michael's nature is to be stupid and romantic, and he follows his nature to the end of the movie.

Background: *If I Die Before I Wake* was written by Sherwood King in 1937. At the time he was living in a Chicago guesthouse and could not afford the rent, so he made a bet with his landlady – each week he would read to her other guests a chapter of the book he was writing, and if they could not solve the mystery he would not have to pay the rent. He went rent-free.

Welles was touring his enormous theatre production of *Around the World in Eighty Days* but his costumes were all locked up and he needed $25,000 in two hours to get them out for that evening's performance. He rang up Harry Cohn, and promised to write and direct a film based on a brilliant thriller he had just read called (he looked at the book the cashier was reading) *If I Die Before I Wake*. Cohn sent the money. (The rights were owned by producer William Castle, who became a producer on the film.)

Welles wrote the script in 72 hours (which uses the plot of the book) and Cohn had it budgeted at $2.3 million. With the rough first draft okayed by Cohn, Welles scooted off to Mexico City to scout locations. His major acquisition was to hire the services of Errol Flynn and his yacht Zaca for $1,500 per day, which included lunch for the crew.

Rita Hayworth, Welles' second wife, from whom he was separated, wanted to play the part of the evil woman, so Welles gave it to her. She was Cohn's biggest star, having just had a hit with *Gilda*. They were briefly reunited during the shoot, but their divorce was finalised soon after.

Glenn Anders was out of work and living in Tallulah Bankhead's house when he was summoned to Hollywood by Welles, who only said that Anders would win an Oscar for the part. Arriving on a hospital set, Welles told him to get under the white sheets. As he was lying there, wondering what the film was called, who his character was and why he was playing a dead man, Anders signed a contract.

13 October 1946: Welles, Rita and 32 actors and crew left for location shooting in Acapulco. It was an arduous shoot. Besides the heat, Rita had to swim in crocodile-infested waters. She also had to jump off a rock into the sea – the rock had to be scraped clean of poisonous barnacles. Not only that, but an experienced diver was positioned in the water to ward off deadly barracudas.

17 November 1946: the first day of filming on Errol Flynn's yacht. On the first take, the assistant cameraman died of a massive heart attack. Flynn, as captain of the ship, took control and ordered the body to be sewn up in a sack and buried at sea.

20 November 1946: shooting resumed but the whole day was lost because light reflected up from the sea over-exposed the film. Trying to catch up, they filmed at night – impossible, because as soon as they powered up the massive arc lights, a swarm of insects descended upon them.

23 November 1946: Flynn's pregnant wife left for LA to have the baby. Flynn disappeared so they could not film on the yacht. Four days later, Flynn returned with an exotic woman in tow – filming resumed.

30 November 1946: the President of Mexico visited and Flynn introduced the exotic woman as William Castle's wife.

5 December 1946: at two in the morning, Welles called Castle, moaning – an insect had bitten him in the eye, which had gone red and grown to three times its normal size. Shooting was suspended.

10 December 1946: cast and crew left for LA, only a couple of days over schedule.

In Hollywood, Welles worked quickly but was edgy and argumentative, and complained about a lack of sleep. The funhouse was designed and painted, then repainted by Welles walking around, brush in hand, his valet Shorty holding the pot of paint. On the Saturday afternoon, Welles wanted the set repainted before Monday's shooting. Jack Fier, studio production chief, refused. Welles and his friends broke into the studio, repainted the set and put up a banner: there is nothing to fear but Fier itself. The paint union closed the set and therefore the studio, since no other union would cross the picket line. Fier arranged a compromise with the unions – a paint crew would receive triple pay – and then took the cost out of Welles' pay. As icing on the cake, Fier erected his own banner: All's well that ends Welles. When he saw it, Welles laughed out loud, rushed to Fier's office, embraced him and they were on good terms from then to the end of the shoot on 27 February 1947.

Cohn's chief editor Viola Lawrence was appalled to find no close-ups in the rushes, so Cohn ordered Welles to film close-ups of Rita. When filming was completed, Cohn ran a rough cut. At the end, Cohn offered $1,000 to anybody who could explain it to him. Cohn wanted to restructure the film, so that it would begin with the trial scene, unfold in one long flashback and then return to the trial for the denouement. The idea was dropped when Cohn found out how much it would cost.

Rita had had a huge hit with Gilda, where she had sung 'Put the Blame on Mame', so Cohn thought he should repeat the process on this film. He bought a song and had Welles shoot a singing scene on 10 and 11 March at a cost of $60,000. Then Cohn had the music repeated throughout the picture to get his money's worth.

Although *The Lady from Shanghai* was ready for distribution early in 1947, Cohn did not like it and feared it would harm the reputation of his star. He held it back, waiting for other Rita films to be made and released, before releasing *The Lady from Shanghai* on the bottom half of a double bill in May 1948. It was a financial disaster.

Cohn never forgave Welles for 'ruining' his star. Cohn spread it all over Hollywood that Welles could not make a film on schedule, on budget and, worse, that Welles could not make a film that made money. From that moment on, for all intents and purposes, Welles was excommunicated from Hollywood.

The Verdict: Although Welles' wit and humour come through, and there are some great scenes (Grisby asking to be killed, the 'shark' picnic, the hall of mirrors), the rest of the movie is often just straightforward studio hokum. Glenn Anders gives a great performance. Overall, though, it does not work because we are never inside the head of the narrator. How is that for ironic? 3/5

Macbeth (1948)

'Like fruit pickers, I go where the work is.'

Director, Writer & Producer: Orson Welles

Cast: Orson Welles (Macbeth), Jeanette Nolan (Lady Macbeth), Dan O'Herlihy (Macduff), Roddy McDowall (Malcolm), Edgar Barrier (Banquo), Alan Napier (A Holy Father), Erskine Sanford (Duncan), Peggy Webber (Lady Macduff/Witch), Christopher Welles (Macduff Child), William Alland (Second Murderer), George Chirello (Seyton), Gus Schilling (A Porter), 107 mins

Story: Clouds. A cauldron bubbles surrounded by three witches. A lump of earth is plucked from the cauldron and hands tear at it. An evil doll of Macbeth is made. 'Something wicked this way comes.' It is Macbeth and his best friend Banquo. The witches tell Macbeth that he will become Thane of Cawdor and then King, but his seed will not succeed him. Banquo's children will hold the crown.

When Lady Macbeth reads her husband's letter outlining the prediction, her sensuous breasts swell. She desires power, wants Macbeth to be King. The Thane of Cawdor is beheaded and the first part of the prophecy is carried out – Macbeth is made Thane because of his great battle prowess. If this part is true, then the rest will be also. They plot to kill the King.

Macbeth has doubts about their venture, but Lady Macbeth has no doubts, says he is not a man. Motivated, he kills the King with a dagger but, in shock, brings the dagger back out with him. Lady Macbeth takes the dagger and returns it to the King's chamber, smearing the grooms with blood. When the alarm is called, Macbeth enters and kills the grooms – the obvious suspects.

Now Macbeth is King but he has no sons to carry on his dynasty. He reproaches Lady Macbeth for being barren and refuses to sleep with her. He cannot sleep. 'Macbeth doth murder sleep.' Instead, in guilt, he takes to drink. He is bored with power because there is no conflict to occupy his mind. Then, it occurs to him that the witches said Banquo's seed would rule in the future. Jealous and afraid, Macbeth hires two men to murder Banquo and his son. Sitting in a tree, the two men wait, then fall upon Banquo, smiting him down. They fail to kill his son.

At the feast, an overwrought Macbeth sweats, a shadow over his face. He sees no one at the table, no one but the ghost of Banquo, his best friend. Macbeth overturns the table in rage.

The witches brew and tell Macbeth to beware Macduff and the moving forest. Afraid, Macbeth keeps Macduff's wife and children hostage. In panic, he kills one of the children and then, resigning himself to his fate, kills the rest of them.

The holy man meets with Macduff to tell him that Malcolm and all the clans must join forces to overthrow

Macbeth. Hearing of his family's murder, Macduff has no choice but to march to war. The armies merge and take boughs from the trees as camouflage.

Lady Macbeth is ill. She sleepwalks, washes her hands and reveals all to her nurse and doctor before throwing herself to her death.

The forest comes towards us, the army attacks. Macbeth, the great soldier, slays many and then meets his nemesis, Macduff ('untimely ripped' from his mother's womb). Macbeth is slain, his head chopped off and put on a spike. In his place is the new King, Malcolm, seed of Banquo.

Visual Ideas: People have often said that this is the horror version of *Macbeth*, and they are not wrong. The mists swirl. The lightning crackles. The light falls menacingly on the actors' faces. Dead bodies hang in the background. We see the Thane's execution and Macbeth's head on a spike.

There are also a lot of Sergei Eisenstein influences – people with spears lined up, the shadows of the drummers at the Thane's execution – from *Alexander Nevsky*, *Ivan the Terrible* and *Battleship Potemkin*. The mirror is used to distort the face, as it had been to distort the body of Michael in *The Lady from Shanghai*.

A shot of a hand is followed by a hand-like tree, which has the two murderers crouched within it – they are doing Macbeth's handiwork. In fact, the tree, with its branches, could be seen as a visual metaphor for the whole movie. The witches hold staffs which have two branches at the top – representing the choice that Macbeth has, to make their prophecy come true or not to believe in them. The Christians have crosses. The parading army holds long pikes, like a sea of branches. The bars on the windows are like barbed trees. The army disguises itself as a forest. Macbeth's crown looks like it has thorns coming out of it.

Audio Ideas: The monologues, always difficult to present on film, are shown as whispered voiceovers with the character in close-up – it works really well. When Macbeth dictates a letter to his wife explaining the witches' prediction, it starts with Macbeth dictating the letter, and then cuts to Lady Macbeth reading it. This is such a loud film – when the King is killed there is a storm, and the alarm is a loud bell which rings insistently. The bell also tolls later.

Themes: A man and a woman crave power. In Welles' films women are just as likely to be corrupt as men. A man of power is destroyed. Guilt haunts Macbeth and his wife after their deed. They are driven to destroy themselves.

As a study of the acquisition and deployment of power it tries to echo Sergei Eisenstein's masterpiece *Ivan the Terrible*. However, Welles' attempt is just that – an echo.

Subtext: One of Welles' major changes of the text was his compression of several minor characters into a holy man. This gives the film a very distinct conflict – the pagan witches versus the Christian holy man. This is made explicit in Macbeth, who chooses to believe the witches and make their words become the truth. Macbeth even kills the holy man. Although Macbeth, the agent of paganism, is destroyed, the witches survive, and much evil has been wreaked upon the land.

Background: Early 1947 – Harry Cohn had been bad-mouthing Welles all over Hollywood, saying that Welles had gone over budget and over schedule on *The Lady from Shanghai*. Needing a quick reply, and wanting to make something with class and quality attached to it, Welles decided to turn to his beloved Shakespeare. Welles tried to get a film of *Othello* made. His idea was to rehearse the play in the US, produce it at the Edinburgh Drama Festival and film it on stage in colour. He would then take a month to shoot inserts, work on the soundtrack and complete editing in the UK. With Richard Wilson he worked out a budget of $740,000 and submitted it to Alexander Kórda. Nothing doing, so Welles transferred the idea from *Othello* to *Macbeth*, to be made as a horror film and proposed it to Republic Pictures. Republic bit.

Republic were known for their 'horse operas' – westerns starring the likes of Roy Rogers and Gene Autry. However, they had also been trying to produce some quality films like *Jealousy* (1945) and *Spectre of the Rose* (1946). They gave Welles a budget of $700,000, $100,000 of which Welles was to receive as writer, director, actor and producer.

Welles rewrote his voodoo *Macbeth* stage production. Back in 1936, Welles was made the director of the Negro Theatre Project in New York. Black actors were never given dramatic roles – they were comic relief. What was Welles to do? Welles' first wife, Virginia, came up with the idea of setting *Macbeth* in Haiti. The voodoo *Macbeth* was born with drums, witch doctors, dancing, thunder and lightning. Among the cast was Abdul, a real witch doctor – a dwarf with gold and diamond teeth – who requested and got 12 live goats from which to make his devil drums. A rumour said that anybody touching the drums would die. On the opening night of 4 April 1936, 10,000 people invaded the streets of Harlem and stopped the traffic. There were 144 performances, and it was the first black production in American history for which whites stood in line.

For his Lady Macbeth, Welles cast Jeanette Nolan – they had worked together on the radio – in her first screen role. (In a bizarre casting decision, Welles had his personal valet, the diminutive Shorty, to play Macbeth's valet Seyton.)

On 21 May 1947, Welles and the nine principles went to Salt Lake City, for the Utah Centennial Festival. Welles rehearsed the cast and did six performances in four days, from 28 to 31 May. The running time was one hour and thirty-four minutes – just right for a film. The festival allowed Welles to use the costumes and props in the film production.

Because the shoot was very tight – they only had a 21-day shooting schedule (19 days principal photography and two days of inserts) – Welles decided to record the voices ahead of time with a click track. (Clicks are added to the tape so that people know when their voice is about to start – it was used for musicals so that the lips start on cue and are perfectly synchronised.) With the pre-recorded tape playing, the technicians could shout out orders and the cranes could make all the noise they needed to.

Filming began on 23 June and it was horrendous. The loudspeaker with the pre-recorded voices was horrible to work with.

There was also a second-unit filming. To save time, during the battle scenes some of the camera operators wore reverse costumes and wielded hand-held Eyemo cameras so that both the long shots and close-ups could be filmed simultaneously. Also, Welles was fond of long takes – they ate up script pages – and did several ten-minute takes. With no budget to do any special effects, Welles decided to show Banquo's ghost as a ghost by simply putting a piece of Vaseline on some glass so that he looked blurred.

John Wayne could be spotted in the wings watching Welles at work. There was also a more pungent reminder of the western pictures – the set reeked of equine urine. At one point, Welles' daughter Christopher, who had a part as a boy, sneaked to the next stage where they were making another horse opera. Upon her return she promptly asked her father why he didn't make interesting pictures like that.

Filming ended 17 July. Remarkably, Welles brought the film in under budget. Herbert J Yates was very impressed by Welles' little experiment to make a quality picture and had nothing but praise. This praise soon evaporated when Welles left for Italy to act in *Black Magic*, leaving Richard Wilson in charge of editing *Macbeth*. Welles seemed more interested in raising money and scouting locations for *Othello* rather than finishing the film that could repair his Hollywood reputation.

Despite numerous phone calls and voluminous correspondence back and forth with Welles, Wilson could not complete the film, so Republic sent editor Louis Lindsay and the film stock out to Italy on 25 November 1947. Lindsay spent so much time working on *Othello* and other Welles projects, that when he returned to Hollywood on 6 March 1948 *Macbeth* was still not complete.

Welles was having a great time in Italy: directing many scenes of *Black Magic*; having a private audience with Pope Pius XII who wanted to know all the latest Hollywood hot gossip; and eluding gangster Lucky Luciano who was convinced Welles should film his life story. However, he was convinced to return to Hollywood in April 1948 to finish cutting *Macbeth*.

Macbeth was entered into competition at the Venice Film Festival in September. Yet for some political reason he could never quite understand, Welles was ordered by the American Embassy to remove the film from the competition. *Macbeth* was released in some European cities in December 1948, but Republic wasn't happy with the Scottish burr, so they asked for the film to be redubbed into American-English. Richard Wilson began work on this in July 1949 and it took him nine months to get all the recordings complete. At the same time, Welles had been asked to reduce the film from 102 to 80 minutes, which he did. The final version of *Macbeth* was released in September 1950.

A 107-minute version of the film with actors speaking in a Scots burr was found in 1980 and is now widely available.

The Verdict: This looks and feels like a movie shot in 21 days. It is raw, some of the acting is atrocious, and the sets look like stage sets. On the other hand, the adaptation of Shakespeare's ideas is very good, and it has energy. There are some visually stunning shots, which have provided many lesser filmmakers with angles and lighting ideas. The problem is that Welles did not have enough time to execute his ideas properly for them to work as a cohesive and balanced whole. 3/5

Othello (1952)

'2% movie-making. 98% hustling.
That's no way to live a life.'

Director & Co-Writer: Orson Welles

Cast: Orson Welles (Othello), Micheál MacLiammóir (Iago), Robert Coote (Roderigo), Suzanne Cloutier (Desdemona), Hilton Edwards (Brabantio), Nicholas Bruce (Lodovico), Michael Laurence (Cassio), Fay Compton (Emilia), Doris Dowling (Bianca), Joseph Cotten (Senator), Jean Davis (Montano), Joan Fontaine (Page), 90 mins

Story: A funeral. A dead man. A dead woman. A man in a cage, hoisted into the air. What events conspired to this end?

Venice. Othello, a Moor, steals away with his love Desdemona and they are married. The union is opposed by Desdemona's father, Brabantio, but the Senate allows it. Brabantio forever turns his back on his daughter. The Moor can have her.

Meanwhile, Iago has been telling Roderigo that Desdemona is really in love with Roderigo, not Othello. Amazingly, the dumb, clumsy Roderigo believes Iago.

Upon hearing news of a Turkish force sailing towards them, the Senate dispatch Othello to Cyprus to defeat the Turks. At sea, he defeats them resoundingly.

Iago wants power – he wants what Othello has. To this end, he decides that he will split asunder the love between Desdemona and Othello using their friend Cassio. First Iago gets Cassio drunk while on duty and Roderigo tries to pick a fight with Cassio without success, then a fight ensues in the sewers – Cassio is found out and is stripped of his officer rank.

Iago then suggests to Cassio that he ask Desdemona to put forward a good word (and thus upright Othello shall think ill of his wife and plant the connection between Cassio and Desdemona).

Talking to Othello about jealousy ('that green-eyed monster'), Iago is both friend and confidant. Othello talks of his fears – he is not the same colour or class as those around or above him. Iago hints that Cassio and Desdemona are more than friends.

Othello is angry and when Desdemona tries to soothe his brow with a white handkerchief he throws it down and steps on it as he leaves. Surreptitiously, Iago collects the handkerchief and delivers it, via his wife Emilia, to Cassio's lover.

Angry Othello towers over Iago, on top of the fortress, the sea crashing below them. Iago is afraid for his life, but raises the question of Desdemona's handkerchief and perhaps that it is now in Cassio's hand. Othello demands the handkerchief of Desdemona but she only talks of receiving Cassio to dine.

Iago arranges for Othello to overhear a conversation

with Cassio. Talking about Cassio's girlfriend, Othello thinks they are talking about Desdemona. Othello goes mad, has a fit, now convinced that Desdemona is unfaithful to him.

Othello wakes on a beach. 'Farewell, tranquil mind.'

Now against his wife, when Lodovico arrives and says that Othello is to return to Venice, Othello hits Desdemona and shouts, 'Cassio shall have my place!' He calls her a strumpet and Desdemona is confused.

It is decided that Othello shall strangle his wife and Iago shall assassinate Cassio.

Iago and Roderigo talk – Roderigo is fed up because he has given Desdemona jewels with no reward (Iago has taken them). Now Othello and Desdemona are to go to Venice. Iago, vile man, suggests that if their friend Cassio dies then they must stay. Roderigo agrees and attempts to murder Cassio in the bath house. It goes wrong. Confusion reigns. Iago kills Roderigo.

Othello enters Desdemona's bedchamber. She must die or she will betray him again. He puts out a candlelight with his hand, then snuffs out her life. Placing a white veil over her, he kisses Desdemona.

Confusion; chaos. Emilia explains to the guards that she had delivered the handkerchief, and Iago kills her. Iago is captured. Othello slays himself. 'Here is my journey's end.' He was, 'One who loved not wisely, but well.'

We witness the funeral of Othello and Desdemona, and see Iago being put in his cage.

Visual Ideas: The main visual theme is of the cage, or being trapped. In the opening funeral, we see Iago being put in a cage. In Venice, Desdemona is always shown through a lattice of wood and shadows. The same cross-hatching of wood, stone, iron and shadows reoccurs throughout the film. At the very end, in Desdemona's room, we see the characters through the spiked criss-cross iron window. This shows that from the beginning of their marriage to Desdemona's death by Othello's hand, they are trapped, as Iago is trapped in his cage. This ties up with Iago's line, 'I shall make the net which shall enmesh them all.'

To cover financial restraints, and for effect, silhouettes are often used. The funeral is in silhouette, as is Iago in his cage, a ship on the fortress wall in Cyprus, Othello on the wall as he approaches Desdemona to strangle her.

There is reverse tracking on many shots as the characters talk and walk through the fortress. One tracking shot goes from far away to close-up on Othello roaring. It brings to mind the famous shots George Miller used to zoom in on *Mad Max*. When Othello wakes after his fit, we see the world from his point of view – upside down.

Reflections: the sword fight in the sewer has all the figures reflected in the shallow water; Othello looks at himself in the mirror.

Audio Ideas: The roar of the sea synchronises with the swirl of Othello's cloak when he is towering over Iago.

Themes: Again, we begin with the death of the central character – his funeral. The scene where Othello only hears some of Cassio's dialogue is reminiscent of the end scene in *Touch of Evil*, where Vargas can only hear some of

Quinlan's conversation. The flawed man of power. The acquisition of power by any means possible.

Subtext: Iago is the engine that drives the story and Welles, who studied Shakespeare and knew him inside out, suggested to MacLiammóir that the reason for Iago's ambition was his impotence. Thus, if Iago did not have sexual power, he should have corporal power. Iago tries to achieve his ends by psychological manipulation of his colleagues.

Iago is almost always portrayed as a small man, standing behind, or in the shadow of, another man or object. Yet, he talks into the ears of men, twisting their desires and fears into something he can use for his own ends.

Othello is a passionate man, a hero, someone to be admired. He believes the best of people until he is proved wrong. At heart, he feels inferior because of the colour of his skin and the lowliness of his class. Although his rank and his deeds inspire devotion and love, ultimately Othello feels that Desdemona cannot truly love him. Thus, she would be drawn to somebody of her own class and colour – Cassio. This flaw in Othello is twisted open by Iago with tragic results.

Background: The troubled filming of Othello has passed into legend. Here are a few facts to give you some idea of the persistence needed to make the film.

August 1947: Welles acted in the Hollywood film *Black Magic* in Italy so that he could set up financing and do some location scouting. Italian producer Montatori Scalera said he would back Welles.

11 November 1947: Welles and Rita Hayworth are divorced.

September 1948: with Scalera's money, Welles began filming in Venice with Lea Padovani as Desdemona. It turns out that Scalera wanted to make Verdi's opera, not Shakespeare's play, so the money all of a sudden ran out. Welles decided to play Harry Lime in Carol Reed's film of Graham Greene's story *The Third Man*, and used the money to finance *Othello*. He spent ten days in Vienna doing exteriors and some more time in England doing interiors.

27 February 1949: Micheál MacLiammóir agreed to play Iago, went to Paris to meet Lea Padovani and rehearsed.

7 March: MacLiammóir returned to Paris and found Welles looking for a new Desdemona. 29 March: Welles went to London looking for money and the new Desdemona. 30 March: MacLiammóir travelled to Rome to get his clothes made and fitted.

5 April: Welles in Dublin, where he persuaded MacLiammóir's partner at the Gate Theatre, Hilton Edwards, to play Brabantio. 7 April: Welles went to Morocco to film *The Black Prince*. 9 April: MacLiammóir returned to Dublin.

18 May: MacLiammóir travelled to Paris, then on to Casablanca to find no hotel room waiting for him. 27 May: MacLiammóir went from Casablanca to Spain, France and Rome, where he stayed at Welles' Villa Bottai, and joined fellow actors Bob Coote, Michael Laurence and Betsy Blair (the new Desdemona).

8 June: from Rome to Paris to Casablanca by plane.

From Casablanca to Mogador, Morocco via car. They found Welles eating, and he told all about his problems financing the film. Rehearsals to begin the next day. The main set was a sixteenth-century Portuguese fortress. A cast and crew of about 70. 10 June: the female costumes arrived from Rome but the male ones were delayed indefinitely. They had to make do with what they had. Alterations would take some time, so how could they film without costumes? Welles had a brilliant idea – film the attempted murder of Cassio by Roderigo in a steam bath, hence no need of costumes. Work began on transforming one of the fortress towers. 19 June: 7.30am. Filming began with seven setups, each having between three and fifteen takes. 21 June: MacLiammóir went blind from Klieg Eye (the type of lights used for filming). 22 June: Edwards arrived in bandages having smashed up his brand-new car in France. 25 June: Doris Dowling arrived to play Bianca and burst into tears when a camel nuzzled her neck. 29 June: MacLiammóir still blind but filming – following directions very carefully.

7 July: Safi. Filming scene on rocks where Iago and Cassio discuss Desdemona within earshot of Othello. Place was used for fishing and as toilet by Arabs, so they had to be thrown off the set. 14 July: Betsy sent to Paris on holiday – never heard of again. 17 July: for drunk scene real barrels of wine were issued – good time had by the Jewish extras. 19 July: shooting in Safi. 23 July: shooting with Desdemona in scenes, but no actress actually in shot. 25 July: filming stopped for Welles to go earn some more money. The actors languished in four-star hotels in England, Rome, Paris and Nice.

4 August: most of cast and crew assembled in Venice, Italy. 8 August: MacLiammóir met Welles on street who comments, 'Isn't it awful having no money?' and said that he had a screen test of Suzanne Cloutier as Desdemona. 24 August: filming resumed on the Grand Canal in Venice. 27 August: filming moved on to the Doge's Palace. 28 August: Joseph Cotten appeared as a Senator, satisfying Welles' superstition that Cotten has to be in every film for it to be a success. Joan Fontaine also in scene as Page Boy. During evening shoot of balcony scene, MacLiammóir repeatedly messed up speech by ending at wrong place due to misunderstanding – Welles became aggressive, in a foul, black mood. They made up over dinner. 31 August: Torcello, island off Venice, in cloisters of church, doing scenes of Othello calling Desdemona a strumpet.

4 September: leaving for Rome, the cast's luggage was forgotten, so MacLiammóir and Edwards volunteered to wait for it. As train left, luggage was discovered on board. MacLiammóir and Edwards were put on the wrong train and spent more than 13 hours travelling from Venice to Rome. 7 September: filming at Scalera Film Studios in Rome. 16 September: long scene, reception of Lodovico, where Desdemona walked from afar to big close-up and was slapped by Othello from out of shot. Each time, Cloutier flinched before the blow and her face was suffering. Fed up, Welles said he would cut in the blow another time. She did the shot then he walloped her! Cut. Print. Cloutier cried, and said she knew he was going to do it all along. 18 September: no money. Welles popped out to get some. Cast disappeared to Paris, Dublin etc.

18 October: filming in Tuscania, Italy, in the crypt of an

eleventh-century church that had 28 slender columns. Continue the jealousy scene between Iago and Othello, begun in Mogador. 23 October: filming in Viterbo, Italy, in thirteenth-century disused church which was used for Desdemona's bedchamber. 24 October: Palazzo Papole and the reverse shot of scene shot in Safi in July. 24 October: MacLiammóir's birthday. Broke tooth on toast, spent day at dentist. 27 October: Othello murders Desdemona. 29 October: Welles collapsed. Doctor said he had a bad heart and was not to smoke or drink coffee. He recovered over dinner.

1 November: they returned to Venice. In Palazzo Ducale, Iago spent day walking on tables to get the angle right. Maize thrown to get pigeons up in air. Filmed also at Ca' d'Oro and Doge's Palace. Terribly cold but good light. 14 November: Welles to Perugia to scout locations. Shots done in his absence dumped because film was faulty. 18 November: no money again. Cast scattered to the four ends of the Earth.

20 January 1950: cast gathered in Mogador whilst Welles was in Marrakech. 31 January: filming resumed in Mogador. The jealousy scene continues.

9 February: filming in Safi. Back to the rocks. Plane and battleship always in frame. Bad weather. Film stock ran out. 14 February: Mazagan. In fifteenth-century Portuguese cistern they film a continuation of the attempt on Cassio's life. Water not dark enough to reflect giant arches, so dye it black. Edwards directed scenes in preparation for *Julius Caesar* project with Welles (which was never filmed). 19 February: at harbour, MacLiammóir put in cage and hauled up into sky. Scene invented by Welles.

Welles needed a crowd up on a wall, so he got all the tailors working on the film to run about with sardine cans on their heads – to create a reflection and give the impression of helmets. 25 February: return to Mogador. MacLiammóir put in chains and dragged backwards through dirt in shot prior to being put in cage.

7 March: MacLiammóir finished scenes as Iago.

Some minor shooting over the next few months, then editing began.

9 September: Welles finished stage tour of *An Evening with Orson Welles* and used money to resume editing.

1 October to 15 December 1950: stage production of *Othello* toured the UK.

19 May 1952: the finished film premieres at the Cannes Film Festival and wins the prestigious Palme d'Or. Phew!

15 September 1955: *Othello* finally opened in New York, but it is a different version to the one Welles cut.

The Verdict: For all the trouble Welles went through to make this film, none of it shows in the final cut. As ever, the words and scenes whirl, creating a dizzying effect as events spiral out of control. There are standout performances by Welles (as earnest but naive leader), MacLiammóir (sly, practical yuppie) and Coote (dumb fool). The bright texture of the images is still fresh today. 5/5

Mr Arkadin (1955)

'By nature, I am an experimentalist. I don't believe much in accomplishment.'

Director, Writer, Art Director, Costumes & Co-Producer: Orson Welles

Cast: Akim Tamiroff (Jakob Zouk), Grégoire Aslan (Bracco), Patricia Medina (Mily), Jack Watling (Marquis of Rutleigh), Orson Welles (Gregory Arkadin), Mischa Auer (The Professor), Peter van Eyck (Thaddeus), Michael Redgrave (Burgomil Trebitsch), Suzanne Flon (Baroness Nagel), Frédéric O'Brady (Oscar), Katina Paxinou (Sophie), Paola Mori (Raina Arkadin), Robert Arden (Guy Van Stratten), Gert Fröbe (Policeman), 99 mins

Alternative Title: *Confidential Report* (UK)

Story: A king is pleased with his poet and wants to bestow a present on him. He asks his poet, 'What can I give you of all that I have?' 'Anything,' the poet replies, 'except your secrets.'

On 25 December, an empty plane flies over Barcelona airport. Why? This film explains all.

Munich: Van Stratten is looking for Jakob Zouk so that he can complete his confidential report, collect his $15,000 fee and save both their lives. Zouk has just been released from jail and does not want to know. Van Stratten tells him the whole story…

Naples: night, the docks, a chase between two men. Bracco is knifed, falls and wants revenge for his death. Bracco tells Van Stratten and Mily that they can earn a fortune – he tells Mily his dying words. The other man, a peg-leg, shoots at the police, is shot and falls dead into the water. Van Stratten is arrested by the police for trying to smuggle cigarettes. What did Bracco say? 'Arkadin, Gregory Arkadin.'

Released from prison, Van Stratten pursues the incredibly rich Arkadin and decides to reach the elusive millionaire through his daughter Raina. After meeting her at a club, she is collected by the invisible Arkadin. Van Stratten meets Mily, now part of Arkadin's party crowd, and they decide to blackmail Arkadin together – if only Mily could remember the other name Bracco told her.

Spain: Van Stratten gets a lift to Spain with Raina, watched by Arkadin's personal secretaries, who are Arkadin's private spy network. 'The Ogre,' she calls her father, like a monster in a nursery rhyme, up in his castle. At a religious ceremony that night, Raina explains that the penitents wore chains and walked barefoot because they were sorry for their sins. 'They must be awful sorry,' Mily comments.

Raina and Van Stratten spend the week together, chasing, flirting, until they kiss.

Arkadin's party in the castle is a masquerade, with many

of the guests wearing Goya masks. Arkadin introduces himself to Van Stratten, leads him to Raina's room and shows him the confidential report he has assembled on Guy Van Stratten, or should that be Streetheimer? Angry, Van Stratten says that somebody should do a confidential report on Arkadin – what secrets would people find out about him?

Storming out, Van Stratten goes to Mily, who says she remembered the other name Bracco told her: Sophie.

Arkadin summons Van Stratten and hires him, for a $15,000 fee, to prepare a confidential report about Arkadin's past. Arkadin is undergoing an intelligence check by the United States Army. On the basis of the information they gather, he may be given a contract to build an Army air force base in Portugal. If Van Stratten, with his underworld connections, cannot find any dirt on Arkadin, then nobody can. Arkadin says he has amnesia and cannot remember what happened before he turned up in Zurich during the winter of 1927, in a suit containing 200,000 Swiss Francs – the basis of his fortune.

Van Stratten takes the job, hoping to find information with which he can blackmail Arkadin. He travels back and forth all over Europe and interviews the Professor in Copenhagen. The Professor, who has a flea circus, knew Arkadin in Warsaw and says that the past is the past – 'Crooks aren't the worst people in the world, just the stupidest – the fleas of the world.'

Tangiers: Mily, followed by Arkadin, meets Thaddeus and gets the name Trebitsch.

Amsterdam: Van Stratten interviews antiquarian Burgomil Trebitsch and finds out that Sophie was the head of a white slavery gang – they sold girls to South America, using a dance academy as a cover. The academy was infiltrated by girls working for the police and the gang broke up – one of the girls was part of the Resistance during the war and is now the Baroness Nagel in Paris.

On the boat, Arkadin and Mily kiss. Mily is drunk and tells Arkadin that they know so much: in 1927 a tailor noticed that Arkadin's suit was made in Warsaw; the Nazis gave him money because of his South American connections; he built roads for Mussolini and men died. The next morning, a woman's naked body lies dead on a beach.

Paris: Arkadin has dinner with the charming Baroness Nagel who says that criminals with money are no longer considered criminals. She knows Sophie's address and, finding the idea of selling information repulsive, instead makes a bet with Arkadin. He settles the bet.

Van Stratten returns to his Paris hotel and meets Raina in the lobby. She wonders why he has been avoiding her – he promised not to work for her father. Entering Van Stratten's room, they discover Arkadin waiting – he is outraged at Raina's impropriety. Van Stratten says he is good enough for Raina – 'Maybe I'll end up an Arkadin myself.'

Mexico: Van Stratten interviews Oscar, a drug addict and former member of the gang, then meets Sophie, now married to a general. She is still sharp, asking if the peg-leg man in Naples had a gun, why did he knife Bracco? Sophie takes out an old photo album and says that she remembers her Alphabasi, as he was called, that she was crazy in love with him and did not really mind the $200,000 in gold he stole from her. The past is the past and should be left alone.

Before Van Stratten leaves the country, he is surprised to meet Arkadin. 'You're the villain,' Van Stratten snarls. But Arkadin says he has a conscience, unlike Van Stratten.

Munich: on his way to Jakob Zouk, Van Stratten is waylaid by some amusing policemen and goes to Arkadin's Christmas party – Arkadin is dressed as Santa Claus. Van Stratten discovers Mily is dead, then finds out Sophie and Oscar have been murdered – their throats cut. A knife whizzes past him, thrown by Arkadin, into a target.

Having told his story, Van Stratten explains to Zouk that whoever knew Arkadin in the past ends up dead, and that he himself will also end up dead. The reason? Arkadin is afraid that his precious daughter Raina will find out about his unsavoury past.

Van Stratten tries to save Zouk, but fails – he finds Zouk with a knife in his back. He is followed by Arkadin, and says he is going to tell Raina and save his own neck. It is Christmas Eve, the flight to Barcelona is full and Van Stratten has a seat. Arkadin stands helpless – nobody will accept his offer of money for a seat. Desperate, he flies a private plane, but Van Stratten gets to Raina first. Over the radio, she tells her father she knows all about him. There is no reply, only an empty plane remains, circling the sky above them.

Raina is distraught. 'Once, a long time ago,' explains Van Stratten, 'he was somebody like me.'

Visual Ideas: The first image of Jakob Zouk looks like a

ORSON WELLES

George Grosz sketch; the peg-leg walking, his shadow on the wall like *The Cabinet of Dr Caligari*; the backlit train and demon smoke; the castle always in the background when Raina and Van Stratten talk; they flirt through the prison-like trees, pillars and walls; the procession of the penitents in tall hats; Arkadin always tall, big, towering over, looking down at Van Stratten, and Van Stratten small, looking up; Arkadin as a black figure between Raina and Van Stratten whenever the three are in the same frame; the Professor working his flea circus in a circle, with a white circle above him, echoes the white circle above Arkadin when he talks to Baroness Nagel, and his white sailor hat when he towers over Mily; the fleas (criminals) feeding off the Professor, just as Van Stratten feeds off Arkadin; to show drunkenness and boat movement, Arkadin is still in the frame while the background moves back and forth; Van Stratten in black, Arkadin in white; the camera moving through the Munich Christmas party; and it goes on and on.

At moments, the mannered style of editing and performance is reminiscent of Sergei Eisenstein's *Ivan the Terrible*, another examination of power.

Themes: Begins with death of central character – the empty plane. The secret to be investigated: how and why did Arkadin die? Man caught in web: Van Stratten is a man who deliberately entangles himself in Arkadin's web, and then regrets it. Clinging to innocence: the corrupt Arkadin only has one part of him that remains innocent – his daughter. Self-destruction: Arkadin sets a chain of events in motion that ultimately leads to his downfall.

Many names: everybody has more than one name, or their name is misheard, misspelt. Masks: Arkadin and Van Stratten hide their true motives and nature. There is the masquerade. Later, Arkadin wears a Santa Claus mask and costume. He is also a sailor, and a pilot. Black & White: Van Stratten wears complete black when he comes out of jail, and in Mexico, in contrast to the white of Arkadin. The failure of power: at the airport, all Arkadin's wealth and position cannot get him a seat on the plane. He calls out, offering lots of money to save himself, rather like Richard's 'My kingdom for a horse'. Mephistopheles: Van Stratten makes a deal with the devil, or at least Arkadin looks like him. *Faust?*

Subtext: Arkadin tells two stories at the party in Spain. The first is about a graveyard, the second about a scorpion and a frog.

Arkadin had a dream that he was in a graveyard where all the dates on the stones were for only a short time. 'Here,' an old man explained, 'we value friendship more than anything else,' and the dates represent the length of friendships. This is a curious story because, first, the length of time is short, and, second, all the friends are dead except the old man. Having seen the film, it is clear that Arkadin is the old man, and all his friends are dead, killed by his own hand. Arkadin then toasts his friends.

Arkadin tells another story: a scorpion wanted to cross a river, so he asked the frog to carry him. The frog refused because the scorpion would sting him. That would not be logical, explained the scorpion, because if he stung the frog they would both drown. So the frog agreed to carry the scorpion. Halfway across, the frog felt a terrible pain – the scorpion had stung him. There is no logic in this, exclaimed the frog. I know, replied the scorpion, but I cannot help it – it is my character.

This is the story of a man who cannot change his nature. Arkadin is a scorpion, who sends out frog Van Stratten to find out what he can about Arkadin. (When the bargain is struck, Arkadin toasts, 'Here's to character.') By killing his past, Arkadin is attempting to change his nature. However, the act of killing reinforces the fact that his nature has not changed.

Why does Arkadin wish to keep his nature hidden? Because he wants to remain a pure figure for his innocent daughter – his vanity demands that he is well thought of by his daughter. The irony is that his daughter is anything but innocent – she spends her time going out with men and does not think well of her father, constantly referring to him as 'the ogre'. Unable to accept a world where the person he thinks most of does not think well of him, Arkadin commits suicide.

Between Van Stratten and Arkadin, who is the worse monster? Arkadin may be corrupt, but he at least has a part of him that remains innocent and pure. Van Stratten, on the other hand, seems to be totally corrupt – he does not seem to care too much about Mily, whom he asks to be with Arkadin – and he is only interested in money and blackmail. It is made pretty explicit that Van Stratten is what Arkadin used to be. This gives the race against time an extra meaning.

In the end, Van Stratten wants to save his own neck. Still, he doesn't tell Raina Arkadin's secret. This hints that there may indeed be something decent within him, something pure and innocent. Perhaps there is hope for Van Stratten, after all.

Background: In August 1951, Welles began writing and performing in a radio series based on his character from *The Third Man*, resurrected by an enterprising producer as *The Adventures of Harry Lime*. Welles was called upon to record the episodes wherever he was in the world. At ten o'clock one morning, Welles summoned puppeteer and actor Frederick O'Brady to his Paris hotel and told him to assemble an English-speaking cast by three that afternoon. O'Brady succeeded, and they recorded *Greek Meets Greek*, written by Welles, featuring O'Brady as the villain of the piece, Gregory Arkadin. Welles promised that he would make a film of the story one day, and take the part of Arkadin for himself.

Greek Meets Greek and another Lime story, which begins with a dying man passing on a secret on the docks of Marseilles, were stitched together by Welles for a proposed film. He finished the script in Rome on 23 March 1953, and called it *Masquerade*. Eventually, through producer Louis Dolivet (publisher of *Free World*), Welles managed to get backing from a group of Spanish and Swiss bankers.

Countess di Girfalco, whose parents were part of the Italian diplomatic service in Africa, used the stage name Paola Mori. Welles had met her whilst she had been acting in an Italian film with Errol Flynn. Determined to get her ready for her leading role in *Mr Arkadin*, he sent her to Dublin for English lessons from Micheál MacLiammóir and Hilton Edwards.

Robert Arden had worked on the Harry Lime radio show with Welles, who had promised him a leading role in a film. Whilst playing in *Guys and Dolls* at the Coliseum in London, Arden got a phone call from Welles during the intermission, saying that Welles was waiting for him in Madrid. Welles' UK representative would contact him and take care of Arden's contractual obligations. At eight the following morning, Sir Carol Reed rang, invited Arden to breakfast, and the arrangements were made. Four days later, Arden arrived at his Madrid hotel, was summoned to dinner at Welles' hotel and found the rest of the cast there. They rehearsed after dinner, finishing at 2.30am, when Welles announced they were to begin filming at 2pm that afternoon. Welles stayed up all night to rewrite their dialogue so that the story would be told in flashbacks.

Filming began in Madrid early in 1954, and the cast and crew travelled around Spain before moving on to Munich, Paris and Rome. Throughout the shoot Welles would rewrite, whilst Dolivet would disappear to Switzerland to obtain more money. As usual, Welles had the occasional outburst on set whilst 'playing director', but he had the charm and genuine remorse needed to bridge any chasms he had created.

After eight months filming, Welles was given a deadline of 2 September to complete dubbing and editing so it could be at the Venice Film Festival – the most important sales arena in Europe. Welles wanted to dub and edit in Paris but this turned out to be a mistake – French customs insisted on stamping the beginning and end of each piece of film and sound tape, no matter how small. This delayed matters by two days – a vital delay. To save time, Welles dubbed the voices of O'Brady, the dead man on the dock, and Mischa Auer's flea trainer, doing superb imitations. He allegedly did 15 parts, including the Munich airport announcer. It was all for naught.

Having missed Venice, Welles began cutting the film together in Rome. Then he missed the 25 December deadline, so Louis Dolivet took the film away from Welles and asked Renzo Lucidi to finish the editing. Welles sent Lucidi instructions, but the flashback format was removed and the narrative made linear.

As always, Welles was looking for money, so Wolf Mankowitz arranged for a French newspaper to serialise *Mr Arkadin* beginning February 1955. Maurice Bessy was brought in to ghostwrite the story, which was then collected as a novel, published in France, anonymously translated into English and mysteriously appeared on both sides of the Atlantic with Welles' name on it. He did not write a word.

The world premiere of the Spanish version of *Mr Arkadin*, which contained a few different actors, was in Madrid during March 1955. The UK premiere, as *Confidential Report*, was on 11 August, whilst the French had to wait until 2 June 1956 to see it. Dolivet sued Welles for approximately $700,000 for his behaviour during shooting, and the court case dragged on for years, preventing US distribution. A version was eventually premiered in New York on 12 October 1962.

In France, *Mr Arkadin* once got into the top 12 films of all time, but it remains largely unseen in the English-speaking world. There are presently four versions of the film available – two American, one English and one

Spanish. I have used the English version for my analysis, which contains one long flashback. According to Welles, his version (which we will never see), begins with the naked body of a dead woman being washed up on a beach, then has Van Stratten telling Jakob Zouk about Arkadin in a series of flashbacks. We often return to Van Stratten and Zouk, who reinforce the plot twists before the final denouement. Welles also said that there were a couple of missing scenes, and one version has 14 minutes missing. Welles refused to talk about the experience, describing the making of *Mr Arkadin* as 'anguish from beginning to end'.

Orson Welles and Paola Mori married on 8 May 1955.

The Verdict: If you had another actor in the place of Robert Arden, the film would be vastly improved. Arden is one-dimensional and does not imbue Van Stratten with any of the subtlety or ambiguity needed for the part. There are many fine visuals, Welles' speeches are spot-on, and there is a wealth of character actors using their considerable skill, especially Akim Tamiroff. If Welles had cut it as he wanted, and with a bit of recasting, it would have undoubtedly been worth more than 3/5.

Touch of Evil (1958)

'Acting is like sculpture.'

Director & Writer: Orson Welles

Cast: Orson Welles (Hank Quinlan), Charlton Heston (Ramon Miguel 'Mike' Vargas), Janet Leigh (Susan Vargas), Joseph Calleia (Pete Menzies), Akim Tamiroff ('Uncle Joe' Grandi), Joanna Cook Moore (Marcia Linnekar), Marlene Dietrich (Tanya), Ray Collins (Adair), Dennis Weaver (Motel Manager), Victor Millan (Manelo Sanchez), Valentin De Vargas (Pancho), Mort Mills (Schwartz), Mercedes McCambridge (Leader of the Gang), Zsa Zsa Gabor (Nightclub Owner), Joseph Cotten (Police Surgeon), Joi Lansing (Blond), Keenan Wynn (Bit Part), 112 mins

Working Title: *Badge of Evil*

Story: Tick-tock. A bomb is put into the boot of a car in Mexico and it explodes just over the border. It is witnessed by Mike Vargas and his wife Susan, who are on their honeymoon. Vargas has just caught a druglord called Grandi and is prosecuting him in Mexico City. 'This could be very bad for us,' Vargas says. He decides to stay and

100

help, and sends Susan back to the hotel. Detective Hank Quinlan arrives on the scene with the rest of the force. Linnekar is the dead man. Zita is the dead blonde. Dynamite was used. Motive unknown. Quinlan's leg gives him his hunches as to what is the truth and what is not.

On the way back to her hotel, Susan is waylaid by a handsome Mexican she names Pancho, is surrounded, and taken to see Uncle Joe Grandi. As he looks at himself in the mirror, Grandi tries to threaten her, saying that Vargas is to drop the Grandi case in Mexico City or else, but she is unmoved and says he has been seeing too many gangster movies. As she leaves, Grandi licks his lips.

Quinlan, the police chief, etc, all go to the strip joint where Linnekar picked up Zita. Outside, a thug throws acid at Vargas, and Vargas chases after him. Inside, the men are attracted to the women, then Quinlan hears a tune on a distant pianola. Following the sound, he meets his old love Tanya. She has a large cigar in her mouth, he has a candy bar in his. She does not recognise him – 'You're a mess, honey.'

In her hotel room, Susan is undressing when a bright light shines in from a room opposite. Blinded and annoyed, Susan unscrews the light bulb in her room and throws it into the opposite room. When Vargas enters, she says she is leaving for the airport but, when Grandi sends her a photo of her and Pancho snapped outside a hotel, Susan says she will stay in a motel on the American side.

On the way to the motel, they are stopped by Quinlan, who takes Vargas, and Pete Menzies drives Susan to the motel. Quinlan forgets his cane and Pete explains that Quinlan stopped a bullet for him, hence the cane. They are followed by Grandi, but Pete spots him, arrests him and drops off Susan at the Mirador Motel.

Quinlan takes Vargas to a construction site – he suspects the dynamite for the explosion came from there – then to the Sanchez apartment. Sanchez, a shoe clerk, is living with Marcia Linnekar, and Quinlan's intuition tells him that Sanchez is the bomber. Vargas washes his hands and knocks over a shoebox, seeing that it is empty. He leaves to phone Susan, to ensure she is okay, and when he returns finds that Menzies found the dynamite... in the shoebox. When Vargas speaks up, Quinlan is rattled. Quinlan goes off with Grandi, watched by Menzies. Vargas goes off with Schwartz to plot Quinlan's downfall.

Grandi talks Quinlan into setting up Vargas. Grandi says that Susan is being taken care of. (Pancho and a juvenile gang take over the motel, persecute Susan, drug her, then leave her naked in a hotel room so that she thinks the worst. Vargas will be so embarrassed by this, he will have to drop his case against Quinlan.) When Grandi offers Quinlan a drink, Quinlan says he does not drink, then looks down to see that he has already finished drinking his glass.

Quinlan, now drunk, off the wagon again, is found by his best friend Menzies. They talk about the murder of Quinlan's wife by strangulation ('the smart way to kill'), and the fact that Quinlan never found the killer.

Vargas meets the DA and says that Quinlan planted the dynamite – he shows the DA a document that proves Quinlan has dynamite on his ranch. Quinlan crashes the meeting and says that Vargas is using his position to supply his wife with narcotics. Vargas goes to the motel, finds Susan missing, races to town, to Grandi.

A hotel in town. Susan, half-naked in bed, is made to look as though she is on drugs. Quinlan puts on gloves and strangles Grandi. Susan wakes looking up into the dead, staring eyes of Grandi. She screams out the window, Vargas' car driving past unheeding.

Vargas rumbles into the Grandi bar, breaks it up, tells them he is not a cop anymore, that he is a husband now. Then he hears that Susan is in jail, accused of murder, and runs to her, embraces her. Menzies takes Vargas aside, shows him Quinlan's cane, which the police found at the murder scene. They agree to illegally trap Quinlan into a confession – Menzies to wear a wire and Vargas to record it.

Menzies talks to Quinlan in a desolate place, but Quinlan realises he is being betrayed, and shoots Menzies. Crying, he tries to frame Vargas. Seeing the blood on his hands, Quinlan goes down to the river to wash his hands and is shot by the dying Menzies. 'That's the second bullet I've taken for you, partner,' says Quinlan, and falls dead into the river.

Schwartz arrives, telling Vargas that Quinlan was right all along – Sanchez confessed to the bombing. 'He was a great detective.' 'And a lousy cop.'

Visual Ideas: The bravura opening scene starts on a close-up of a bomb, pulls out to see the bomb being put into the boot of a car, and the car driving four blocks to the border, before being blown up. The first cut is on the explosion; the camera quickly zooms into it. This is done by skip-framing – alternate frames are cut out (by hand) to make the zoom quicker. Then there is a handheld camera sequence as people are running towards the flaming car. All this within the first few minutes.

Other amazing shots include: the Sanchez interrogation scene all done in one take; Schwartz and Vargas in a car going through the town at high speed; the camera swinging up from the ground to a hotel room with a shining torch. When Vargas hears his wife is in jail, Welles blurs the picture going out. There are many lovely touches throughout the movie.

From the beginning, Quinlan is filmed from below to make his already enormous bulk seem monumental. The only time he seems weak is when he hears the pianola music. The first time he looks small is in the scene where Grandi persuades Quinlan to frame Vargas – the pianola music is on in the background and Quinlan drinks.

As for editing... when people talk, Welles cuts between them so that you see the expressions and reactions of all the participants. He also cuts from one sequence to another, so that everything is happening in parallel – you have no time to breathe.

There are many uses of signs within the movie: when Vargas goes to investigate the explosion the billboard behind him says 'Welcome Stranger'; when Vargas phones Susan from a shop run by a blind woman, behind him can be seen the sign, 'If you are mean enough to rob the blind, help yourself'; after Quinlan kills Grandi, he leaves the room and the sign on the door clearly states, 'Stop. Have you left anything?', and of course Quinlan has forgotten his cane; and when a Mexican thug throws acid at Vargas, he misses and burns an image of Zita, the blonde dancer who was killed in the opening explosion.

Reflections are used throughout to show more than one thing at a time. As Vargas goes into a shop, in the window we see Menzies and Grandi arriving in a car. When Quinlan and Grandi are leaving together, we see Pete Menzies looking at them through the window, and their reflection in the window. We then cut to a window reflection of cars arriving at the motel.

Audio Ideas: For the music, Welles asked Henry Mancini to use natural sounds, like rock and roll music from radios, and the music for Tanya's pianola, which give the film a bleak feel. The pianola music is used as Quinlan's conscience – it is his sensitive side. When Susan is drugged the music is deafening – welcome to David Lynch territory.

As the wiretap is in operation, Welles brilliantly tunes in and out creating multiple meanings to the dialogue, keeping us on edge. And the 'Guilty, guilty, guilty' repeating at the end is an echo of the end of *Brighton Rock*, where the record Pinky leaves for his girlfriend constantly repeats, 'I love you.'

Themes: Loss of Integrity; The Big Man Falls; Betrayal of Friends.

Subtext: The central question is, 'Who is the boss – the cop or the law?' (In many ways, this is a similar theme to *The Trial*, since Quinlan abuses and manipulates the law.) *Touch of Evil* is about the decline and fall of Quinlan, as witnessed by Vargas.

Quinlan is fascinating because of his moral ambiguity.

As Renoir said, 'There is no one who doesn't have his reasons.' The more human Welles makes Quinlan, the more interesting he becomes. The most complex character in the movie, he is both good and bad. On the plus side, he loves Tanya, he stopped a bullet for Menzies and he knows from experience who is innocent and who is guilty. On the minus side, he is sometimes both judge, jury and executioner. A great detective and a lousy cop.

The death of Quinlan's wife obviously sent him over the top – he could not find his wife's killer and turned to drink. (When Quinlan kills Grandi it has a sexual feel to it, with Susan's groaning and writhing. Symbolically, Quinlan is killing the man who murdered his wife.)

Vargas is transformed by the experience. At first, he is a straight cop, whiter than white, who hates the fact that he has to do the job. 'A soldier doesn't like war.' Then, when Susan is kidnapped, he breaks up the Grandi bar and declares, 'I'm no cop now.' He then uses evil means to trap Quinlan, so he is becoming as bad as Quinlan and betraying the law. Similarly, Menzies betrays his friend Quinlan, the man to whom he owes his life.

Background: In 1956, Eddie Muhl, head of Universal International, bought the rights to the hardboiled novel *Badge of Evil* by Whit Masterson and allocated Albert Zugsmith as producer. Zugsmith asked Paul Monash to write a script in four weeks, which he then didn't care for and it got put on a pile.

In December 1956, Muhl suggested Charlton Heston for the lead in *Badge of Evil*. When Heston got the script, Zugsmith asked who he thought should direct. Heston, who was a big star and whose opinion carried weight, said Orson Welles was playing the heavy, so why not ask him? Zugsmith says that because he knew Welles from the shoot of *Man in the Shadow* (1957), he offered Welles a script to direct. Welles asked, 'Which is the worst?' Zugsmith gave him *Badge of Evil* and two weeks to rewrite it. Welles took 17 days.

Welles used some of the Monash script, put in more scenes from the novel, and then added themes and scenes of his own. There are differences – for example, in the novel Vargas' wife is Mexican, and Welles invented Tanya, the night clerk, and other characters.

Welles could not get the authentic Mexican locations he craved. Aldous Huxley suggested that Venice, California would be a suitable location. Once Welles saw it, he was convinced and rewrote the end to take place on the bridge.

The studio gave Welles Charlton Heston, Janet Leigh and a budget of $895,000. The rest was up to him. Joseph Cotten, Marlene Dietrich, Mercedes McCambridge and Keenan Wynn all agreed to work for union-scale wages, without credit, simply to be in a film with Welles. Since Welles was having all his friends in it, Zugsmith got his friend Zsa Zsa Gabor a cameo as well.

At the time, Welles weighed 270 pounds but to play Quinlan he wanted to be even bigger. He added 60 extra pounds with a false stomach and hump. He acquired a new nose and jowls. He also had a cane because he limped – Quinlan had stopped a bullet for Menzies.

Welles met Heston on 14 January 1957 and they talked about the film. Then, between 22 and 26 January, Welles cut 25 pages from the script (scenes which Zugsmith said would bore the kids) to make the final draft. Rehearsals began on 9 February for nine days.

This was Welles' first Hollywood film in ten years and he had to show that he was reliable, that he could get the film completed within the budget and on schedule. The studio would have their spies on set and they would be waiting for him to fail.

18 February. 9am. First day, first scene. Welles got the first shot at 9.15am, and the second at 9.25am. They were inserts. The studio spies reported back. The studio was happy. Then Welles, assisted by cinematographer Russell Metty, blocked out the Sanchez interrogation scene so that it could be done in one shot. Nothing was shot for hours, as Welles rehearsed the camera going through three rooms with breakaway walls and choreographed the seven speaking parts and extras. The studio was in a sweat. 6.25pm. Welles does the whole scene in one shot. Twelve pages of script. Two days ahead of schedule.

19 February. Second day, out in Venice. Two cars, one with a camera, the other with Vargas and Schwartz. Zooming through alleys, the actors talk through 13 pages of script. Welles said, 'Now that we've taken care of the front office, we'll go ahead and make our picture.'

As filming progressed, the studio loved the rushes and talked about a four- or five-picture deal. Welles thought he was back in favour, that he would be making one movie after another. To celebrate his return, Welles threw a party for all influential Hollywood moguls. Returning from filming, still wearing his grotesque make-up and clothes, all the bigwigs shook his hand vigorously and said he never looked so good!

Janet Leigh did the whole film with a broken left arm – it was in a cast most of the time, heavily disguised, covered or not shown. She was not the only one injured. Whilst filming in Venice, Welles fell into a canal and hurt his ankle so badly he really did need the cane. The injuries were extensive. His face was bruised, but that was covered with make-up. He sprained his wrist, ankle and knee. When not in front of the camera, Welles sported an arm-sling and splint.

There were many night shoots, but somehow Welles would find the energy to stay up and rewrite the script during the day. This energy and determination was shown in the way he treated the actors. Welles loved Dennis Weaver in the TV show *Gunsmoke*, so wrote the character of the night clerk specifically for him. Weaver only had three days away from the TV series; Welles closed down the set so that he could have more time to discuss and develop the character with Weaver.

Marlene Dietrich was an old friend of Welles and wanted to be in his movie. Welles said he wanted a dark look for her, so she visited the studios, borrowing the black wig from *Golden Earrings*, and other costume parts from *Rancho Notorious* (director Fritz Lang) and *Stage Fright* (director Alfred Hitchcock). Welles did not tell the studio that he had Dietrich in the movie. When they saw her in the rushes they immediately paid her more money so that they could put her name on the advertising.

On 14 March, for the long opening sequence – a bravura crane shot over four blocks – they were up all night rehearsing and filming. Each time something would go wrong, usually the guard who had to say his lines at the end. Eventually, the sun was about to rise, and on the last shot they got it.

Unbeknownst to Akim Tamiroff, for his death scene Welles had ordered some lamb tongues for Tamiroff to put in his mouth. Tamiroff overcame his revulsion and put it in his mouth. The fraction of a second cut was too gory, so it was not used. Instead, Tamiroff wore contact lenses with bulging eyes.

The last scene was filmed on the last day of the shoot, on 2 April, then the editing began. Most of the movie was edited with Virgil Vogel, then Edward Curtiss came on board for a short time before being replaced by Aaron Stell on 6 June. By this stage, Welles was asked to stay out of the editing room, as was Hollywood practice, so he watched the film in a projection room and wrote notes that Stell followed. Some post-production photography was needed, so Welles did that.

Eddie Muhl wanted to see the film, so the executives were shown a rough cut on 22 July, which they did not like. Welles was crushed by their critical comments. They loved the rushes, so why did they not like the film? He could see his five-picture deal evaporating. What did he have to do to convince these people?

Ernest Nims, a Universal executive with an editing background – he had worked with Welles on *The Stranger* – was brought in to edit the film with Welles. On 28 August, Nims ran a recut version for Welles, who thought it was good but that it needed a few minor changes. Universal waited for three weeks but heard nothing. Welles said the changes had been lost in the post, but when they still did not arrive, Universal decided to shoot a few additional scenes for clarity. Muhl was becoming disheartened with Welles' attitude.

On 4 November, ten weeks late, Welles' nine-page memo arrived. Half of the 40 last-minute suggestions were carried out by Nims. One of the major things Welles wanted was for the credits to go at the end of the movie so that the audience wouldn't be distracted from the long opening shot.

Universal decided that, in the interest of clarity, extra scenes were to be shot. Welles offered to write and direct them for free but was refused because now Universal did not think Welles was reliable. Director Harry Keller and cinematographer Cliff Stein were told to duplicate Welles' style as best they could. Welles was desperate to stop what he considered to be a butchering of the film. He wrote to Heston, who cancelled the shoot on 18 November at his own expense ($8,000). Heston was persuaded by Universal and it was all done on 19 November.

The following scenes were filmed: four short scenes between Vargas and his wife in the hotel (less than a minute); Vargas and Susan's love scene in the car; Quinlan and Menzies meeting Vargas en route to the motel (Welles was not in the scene – a stand-in was used and Welles dubbed it); Menzies explaining to Susan about Quinlan's leg (Keller had to shoot this because otherwise Quinlan's final line – 'That's the second bullet I took for you, partner' – does not make sense). The dialogue for these scenes were written by Frankie Coen.

Heston rang Welles to let him know what scenes had been filmed, and when Welles saw the Keller footage edited into the film he replied immediately with a 58-

page document. About half of these comments were adhered to. For example, Nims put back in the longer scene between Vargas and the night clerk at the motel, and also kept in the tape playback of 'Guilty, guilty, guilty' at the end.

Welles thought that Nims had improved some parts, but the main thrust of Welles' argument was regarding style. Welles wanted a fragmented style, with more jumping between scenes/locations, whereas the studio wanted a smooth, linear continuity as was customary during that period. Welles' purpose in using this style was to create an atmosphere of nightmare and strangeness, whereas the new scenes and studio editing made it seem more normal.

Upon its release in February 1958, there was hardly any publicity, no press showing, and *Touch of Evil* played as the B picture on a double bill. Universal may well have been afraid of the movie and for a good reason – they were in financial trouble, had suffered heavy losses and were in danger of being shut down. Far from butchering *Touch of Evil*, Universal were probably more concerned with getting some money back from their investment. Ironically, they actually released Welles' short version, and when the 'long' version with Keller's footage was found in 1981, many proclaimed this as the long-lost 'uncut' Welles version.

Touch of Evil got bad reviews in America, and good ones in Europe. On 8 June 1958 it won film of the year in Brussels, and played the whole winter in Paris. In 1998, a re-edited and restored Director's Cut was released based on Welles' 58-page memo.

The Verdict: Since its release *Touch of Evil* has remained a firm favourite of film noir enthusiasts and has recently been renovated to classic status by 'respectable' critics, which is the least it deserves. Great from top to bottom, and from beginning to end, this has terrific performances from Welles and Calleia, and some of Welles' most assured direction. 5/5

The Trial (1963)

'A film is a ribbon of dreams.'

Director, Writer & Co-Editor: Orson Welles

Cast: Anthony Perkins (Joseph K), Arnoldo Foà (Inspector A), Madeleine Robinson (Mrs Grubach), Jeanne Moreau (Miss Burstner), Orson Welles (Advocate), Maydra Shore (Irmie), Suzanne Flon (Miss Pittl), Max Buchsbaum (Examining Magistrate), Carl Studer (Man in Leather), Max Haufler (Uncle Max), Romy Schneider (Leni), Akim Tamiroff (Block), William Chappell (Titorelli), Michel Lonsdale (Priest), Paola Mori (Librarian), Katina Paxinou (Scientist [scenes deleted]), 118 mins

Story: We assume that the law is accessible to all. A man wants to access the law and seeks it at the castle. He goes to an open gateway and the guard tells him to wait. The guard accepts bribes and, as the years pass, the man becomes old and enfeebled, but still he is not allowed to pass through the gate. Near death, the old man asks a question of the guard: 'In all the years I have been here, why have I never seen any other people attempt to pass through this gate?' 'Because,' the guard replies, 'this gate was meant only for you, and now I am closing it.' The guard closes the gate, and the old man dies.

A small, box-shaped room. A man walks through the door from Miss Burstner's room and wakes Joseph K. The man asks questions, and K is embarrassed by the invasion into his personal space – K is trying to dress. Another man enters. They are the police, and they have come to arrest K. 'What is the charge?' They do not say. 'Who accuses me?' K finds three of his colleagues in Miss Burstner's room. K throws them out, and tries to continue his breakfast, moving from one room to the other, never getting anywhere. Two of the detectives say they want to take his record collection, because all his possessions will be impounded and he will never see them again anyway. K makes a complaint about the way he is being treated and the Inspector – the man who woke him – says that now it is serious if he is making an official complaint.

The detectives leave and Miss Burstner returns from work (she is a dancer and drinks with the clients afterwards – the landlady thinks she has no moral fibre). K is infatuated with her. K says that he always feels guilty, even when he is not. Nobody is completely innocent in their mind, Miss Burstner teases, at which K kisses her.

At work, hundreds of people are typing, and well-dressed K moves through them quickly. K puts a cake on a shelf in the storage cupboard – it is a present for Miss Burstner. His boss sees the cake, makes a suggestive remark regarding K's girlfriend, and says that K is 'a bright young man on the way up'. K is embarrassed that his cousin Irmie has come to see him at work. His boss leers at her, saying that she is a bit young.

Returning home that night, K sees a woman with a brace on her leg dragging a trunk out of the block of flats and through the desolate streets. K has Miss Burstner's cake in his hands and offers to help, but only to be polite. It turns out that the trunk belongs to Miss Burstner, who has been evicted because of K.

At the theatre that night, K is summoned by a note from the police. He follows the Inspector who says they are accommodating K by interrogating him outside his normal working hours. K sees two men, and is told that it is not their job to follow him. The Inspector sends K to see the examining magistrate.

K arrives at the courtroom crammed to the ceiling with people. The examining magistrate and everybody else are waiting for him. K jumps onto the stage and tells them that the cops are corrupt (everybody laughs) and gives a rousing speech, but everybody is paying more attention to the guard and his wife making love at the back of the room.

At work the following day, in the storage cupboard, K finds the two cops who wanted his records being whipped because they were caught being corrupt. K tries to stop the barbarity of it all but fails. Returning to his office, K finds his Uncle Max worried about the charges. K says he cannot have long conversations with relatives during working hours. K hears the noise of the cops being whipped and returns to the storage cupboard to find them putting tape on their mouths so that their screams will not disturb him.

Max takes K to see an old friend, the Advocate, who is in bed being ministered to by sexy nurse Lenny. K sneaks off with Lenny – they fool around and kiss on a pile of paper. K is told he is too stubborn, a trouble-maker, and he must be more co-operative, perhaps even make a confession. As a sort of warning, K sees Block, a client, forlornly waiting for the Advocate.

The next morning K goes back to the courtroom to speak to the examining magistrate directly, but it is empty. Looking through the law books, K finds nude photos. He thinks that the law is corrupt, that people make it difficult because they want to make money out of the situation. The guard's wife comes on to K, saying that she wants him. As she does so, the man who whipped the cops, who it turns out is a law student, kidnaps then delivers the guard's wife to the examining magistrate. K follows and he stumbles around the maze-like structure, where rows of frightened victims wait for judgement. He cannot get out. In the archives, he almost faints, and then is free.

On the steps outside, K meets cousin Irmie, says he is going to dismiss the Advocate, and walks to work. Later, at the Advocate's, K is introduced to Block, a client, who is systematically humiliated by the Advocate. The Advocate reveals to K that Lenny is sexually aroused by accused men and she passes on all the lurid details of her encounters to him. Rudy Block seems to like the situation – 'To be in chains is sometimes safer than to be free.'

Having dismissed the Advocate because he has no faith in his power, K goes to meet the artist, the man who paints the portraits of judges. He is said to have their ear, and may be able to put in a good word for K. K climbs up to the artist in his wooden cage. Talking, the artist says that he only paints lowly judges and could possibly get an ostensible acquittal, but he could be arrested up to four times. K buys paintings to buy the artist's support then runs through tunnels, young girls menacing him, ending at an empty church, talking to a priest, who tells him the parable of the man and the guard at the gateway.

Two cops grab hold of K and walk him to a pit. K undresses, sits, lies down and the two cops pass a knife between them. They rise and begin to walk out of the pit. K shouts at them that he will not kill himself, that they will have to kill him and laughs. They throw a pile of dynamite into the pit and it explodes. The door closes.

Visual Ideas: You need to watch this several times to appreciate just how bizarre, experimental, nightmarish and modern the whole thing feels. Move over David Fincher, Joel Schumacher, Tony Scott and the rest – Welles had all the angles, all the cuts, and all the lighting effects sketched, built, rehearsed, filmed and projected before they were even born.

The interrogation in K's room is a six-minute shot. Welles holds on the characters, making it more and more claustrophobic. (In K's room, there is a picture of Van Gogh's *Sunflowers* on the wall, a sign of madness?) At the beginning, K runs around the claustrophobic labyrinth of his rented room and the adjacent rooms. He can never escape the police even though this is his domain. This echoes the labyrinth of his place of work, and the law courts. In the end, the church is connected to the law, which is connected to the police. It is all connected – it is one giant labyrinth.

At K's workplace, there is a long tracking shot across

850 clacking typewriters in a giant white room that is reminiscent of the rows of desks in a famous shot from King Vidor's *The Crowd*.

The cops being whipped in the storage room is the first actual physical violence in the movie, and it is terrifying, shown as it is with a solitary light swinging wildly, giving a strobe effect.

The Advocate spends all his time in bed, with no paper around him, and yet we find K and Lenny making love on a pile of lawyer briefs, disregarding their importance.

To emphasise the web-like qualities of K's predicament, a copious number of spidery shadows drape the scenery. Also, the network of windows and squares on the ceilings and walls of the modern buildings give a similar feeling of entrapment.

Although the Advocate is large and imposing, the important people that all the victims are trying to meet (the clerk of the court, the examining magistrate, etc) are never seen in close-up and, if they are seen at all, it is always from a great distance.

Visual parallels are made between K and Block. Although K is tall and well groomed, and Block is small and grubby, they appear dressed in the same colours. Block fights the system by being wily and stubborn (he has five advocates), in the same way that K fights it by being obnoxious. Block is desired by Lenny because he is a victim and she obviously grants him sexual favours – something that K desires. This enrages K, so he begins to hurl abuse at Block, and is represented as an imposing figure looming over Block, in the same way that the Advocate later abuses Block.

Audio Ideas: Welles once said that if he feels the audience is falling asleep then he will throw in a loud noise to wake them up. In *The Trial*, he is just as likely to throw in a silence so that the contrast makes the noises seem louder and the silences more deafening. *The Trial* veers wildly between loud and silent, both aurally and visually. Most impressive are the 850 typewriters clattering away, which all stop work together, followed by silence. For most of the film, the voices are low, soft, then a crash of voices – in the courtroom, you can hear a pin drop, K makes his speech and the whole room erupts with laughter, yet is stone silent whilst the guard and his wife make love. This stretching of the big and small is echoed in the pictures, which are distorted like a bad dream – enormous doors, tiny spaces, extreme close-ups, minute figures in a bleak landscape.

Themes: The fable tells us that the film is about a man caught in a web. This not only applies to K but to everybody in the film. Clinging to integrity: at first, it seems that Joseph K is the little man, the man of integrity, but as we listen to him moan about the situation and act improperly, we see that no one in the movie has any integrity at all. So, this is not a theme of the movie, and perhaps the reason why so many Welles fans react against it. Abuse of power: the Advocate uses his position to play with Rudy Block's emotions. Joseph K also bullies Rudy Block. Corrupt authority: when the policemen interview K, they want to take his record collection. The police accept corruption as a natural part of the system. Servile acceptance: all the power exerted by the system is accepted by everybody in the movie except K. In this way, he is the hero. However, he is not a perfect person. He is not a nice man. The screen: the parable is told via a movie projector, so we get a story within a story.

Subtext: Welles always found this film hilarious. To him, Joseph K is guilty of everything. K is an up-and-coming executive, an ambitious man and he deserves everything he gets. K comes on to all the women in the movie – he wants them. He exerts his power over others, as others exert it over him. However, K is so up-and-coming, so fast, that he neatly bypasses all the thousands of other numbered men waiting in fields and in corridors, on his way to his death sentence. This is the blackest of black comedies where the law uses its power to play on people's innate sense of guilt. Welles: 'Kafka hates the law. What I hate are the abuses.'

On another level, *The Trial* is about the inability of man to communicate – either with himself (K does not acknowledge his own motives), with other people (K does not make it clear to women whether or not he loves them) or with society (K fails to convince his work colleagues, the police, the law courts, the Advocate, other victims, or the church of his innocence).

The Advocate (words) and the painter (images) are very similar. They both live in a room with a bed, are ministered to by a wild woman/girls, and claim to have the ear of the judges. They both want to make money out of the system, although there are no guarantees and you may lose anyway.

K is exactly the kind of person who built this world –

he is selfish (will not talk to his family, does not help others), dictatorial, immoral (tries it on with many women), obnoxious (argues with everybody and does not listen to what they say) and ignorant (has to ask questions constantly, because he does not know the world he lives in, which is precisely why it is that way in the first place). K boasts at one stage that he enjoys making petitioners wait for him – he is the reason the world is full of endless queues, yet he complains when he is in the queue.

Yes, this is about paranoia, the totalitarian state in both politics and business, and it is about the oppression of the individual in modern society. In every case, it is a male who is the oppressed and the oppressor. The women have no role in this society – Miss Burstner, the landlady, Irmie, the woman with the brace, the guard's wife, the librarian and Lenny may be associated with power, but never hold it. Or do they? This is a very erotic film. Is it about the seduction of power? The women constantly try to draw K and other men away from the law and the office and that whole power thing, but they never succeed. Even at the end, when K is in the tunnel, surrounded by the screaming teenagers, he is still seeking power.

Background: Welles spent one day in 1959 shooting his scenes for Abel Gance's *Austerlitz* (1960), where he met producers Alexander and Michael Salkind. They gave Welles a list of 15 classic books for him to direct and he picked *The Trial* by Franz Kafka. The Salkinds were so broke that they had to borrow money to visit Welles to discuss the project. Over a period of time, money was secured from mysterious sources in Germany, France and Italy, giving a budget of $1.3 million.

For much of 1961, Welles spent his time writing the script and designing the sets. Kafka wrote *The Trial* in 1923 and it was published unfinished. Even the order of the ten chapters is questionable. Welles decided to take the incidents and rearrange them in his own way, to fashion a new design. Shooting began, in English and French, at the Studio de Boulogne in Paris on 26 March 1962. They moved on to three weeks of locations in Zagreb, which brought out the best in Welles. Everybody was laughing whilst making it and Welles maintains it was the best fun he ever had on a set. This was because there were constant problems, and people had to perform at their professional and emotional best to get the project done. For example, Welles told Perkins that they only had enough film in the camera for two takes of the long opening scene, which made it somewhat nerve-wracking for Perkins. Perhaps one of the reasons for Welles' good humour was because he met Olga Palinkas, the daughter of the film designer. She is a sculptor, actress, TV anchor and writer. Later, rechristened as Oja Kodar, she became Welles' companion and collaborator.

For K's workplace, the production dressed an enormous exhibition hall, with 850 desks, 850 typewriters and 850 typists. They filmed a sequence with the computer that was subsequently cut. The computer knows everything, so K asks it to tell him his future. It tells him his fate... on a line of punched tape that he cannot read.

For the death scene on 27 May, Welles did not think that, post-World War Two, he could show a Jew lie down and accept his death, as Kafka wrote it. So, in the film, Joseph K is defiant to the end.

The law courts had been extensively designed by Welles, but the night before they went to Prague to do the interiors, the Salkinds told Welles that the Yugoslav backers had withdrawn their money. With no money, the whole company skipped town and got on the next train to Paris.

Orson wandered around Paris at night, trying to figure out how and where to film the interiors. He looked up, saw the two clock faces of the Gare d'Orsay and walked around the deserted train station until dawn. He found all the sets he needed for *The Trial*. The Gare d'Orsay was owned by an old woman who agreed to the filming. It is now the Musée d'Orsay, one of the most prestigious art galleries in the world.

Welles moved everybody into the building. The editors had rooms, he slept in the Advocate's bed, the dripping candles provided the light they worked by, they ate on the tables – it was their home as well as their set.

After further short sequences were filmed in Dubrovnik, Rome and Milan, the shoot ended in Paris on 5 June and cutting began immediately.

As was usual for Welles, there were sequences comprised of film shot in different countries. In one scene, K emerges from the Gare d'Orsay in Paris, comes down the steps of the Palazzo di Giustizia in Rome to meet his cousin, strolls by the entrance of a factory in Milan and returns to a council house in Zagreb. It is linked by sound and the rhythm of the cuts. The editing is very severe, quick. As Truffaut said, 'The films of Orson Welles are shot by an exhibitionist and cut by a censor.'

As for dubbing, Welles provides 11 of the voices, plays the Advocate and the narrator, and even dubbed ten lines of Perkins' dialogue – Perkins could not work out which ones they were.

The French-language version had a Paris premiere on 21 December 1962, whilst it was first shown in New York on 20 February 1963. *The Trial* failed both critically and financially. Welles said that people expected Joseph K to be some sort of Woody Allen type, and Anthony Perkins was far more aggressive and obnoxious. The object of Welles' scorn was the corporations and the blithe corruption that is carried out in their name, but critics did not seem to pick up on this.

Welles had complete control from beginning to end – the first time since *Othello*. It was a happy experience for Welles and the film is exactly how he envisaged it.

The Verdict: Of Welles' 13 films, this is probably the most difficult to watch. Not because of the depressing subject matter, but because of the constant bombardment of sound and images which make it harder to interpret and assimilate the information. Unlike other Welles films, it does not have a moral ending. You have to think after the film is finished to find out what it is really about. Repeated viewing makes things clearer, and the film more enjoyable – it is no trial at all. 5/5

Chimes at Midnight (1965)

'Friendship creates only the illusion of not being alone.'

Director & Writer: Orson Welles

Cast: Orson Welles (Falstaff), Jeanne Moreau (Doll Tearsheet), Margaret Rutherford (Mistress Quickly), John Gielgud (Henry IV), Marina Vlady (Kate Percy), Walter Chiari (Mr Silence), Michael Aldridge (Pistol), Tony Beckley (Ned Poins), Jeremy Rowe (Prince John), Alan Webb (Shallow), Fernando Rey (Worcester), Keith Baxter (Prince Hal), Norman Rodway (Henry 'Hotspur' Percy), Beatrice Welles (Falstaff's Page), Ralph Richardson (Narrator), Ingrid Pitt, 115 mins

Alternative Title: *Falstaff* (USA)

Story: Snow. A fat man and a thin man walk into a big hall and sit in front of a raging fire. 'The days that we have seen,' says the big man, Falstaff, 'we have heard the chimes at midnight.'

Flashback to stationary Henry IV and ever-active Hotspur in dispute. Henry IV admires Hotspur for his energy and his concern for the state. If only Henry's son

Prince Hal was a man like Hotspur – Hal spends most of his time drinking, fornicating and worse with Sir John Falstaff.

At the Boar's Head. Falstaff (who has no money to pay Mistress Quickly for his rent) and Hal plan a robbery in the woods. Falstaff gets the money then Hal and his friend Ned, dressed as villains, take the money from Falstaff. Upon his return to the Boar's Head, as expected, Falstaff spins a wild yarn about the hordes of villains needed to unencumber him. Even after Hal and Ned reveal themselves to be the villains, Falstaff sticks to his story. In fun, Hal and Falstaff re-enact scenes between Hal and his father, and then switch roles.

Hal goes to his father and the scene is acted for real. There is a war on – Hotspur wants to rule. Henry tells his son that he is a disappointment. Hal promises to make things right.

Falstaff goes to war. First he picks his fighting men (pathetic) and then assembles for battle. Armoured soldiers are lowered from trees onto horses – Falstaff falls to the ground.

The two sides rush headlong into each other, fog engulfing them. Falstaff lumbers around not knowing what to do, hiding. Men kill brutally and die writhing in the mud. We do not know who is on which side.

Hal and Hotspur meet and duel. Hal kills Hotspur, then cowardly Falstaff claims the kill. This causes a rift between Hal and Falstaff, although Henry IV realises his son may not be so bad after all.

Later, after Falstaff has agonised over his actions and delighted in Doll Tearsheet's love, Hal comes to him and they drink together. But it is not like old times – there is something serious within Hal. Hal returns to his dying father. He claims the crown.

End of flashback. 'All is dead. All is double-dead.' Falstaff says, 'We have heard the chimes at midnight.'

Hal's father wakes, and they are reconciled. The former King passes on some advice to the new King: 'All my friends must be your friends. Beware the stings and talons.' As Hal lifts his new crown, we cut to Falstaff's friends dancing. Falstaff admits that 'old men have the vice of lying', but he is looking forward to making his friend Hal laugh again. His Hal is waiting for him.

At the coronation, Falstaff desperately tries to find his King but his way is barred by a forest of pikes. Eventually, he shouts to Hal in anguish, 'I speak to my heart.' The King turns around and says, 'I know you not', and 'Being awake, I do despise my dream.' The King banishes Falstaff from his sight, upon pain of death. 'Sir,' Falstaff replies to his King, 'I shall be as good as my word.'

As Henry V prepares for war with France, Mistress Quickly tells us that Falstaff is dead – the King broke his heart. A giant coffin is wheeled away. The new King is a new man, a man of prudence.

Visual Ideas: The photography is stunning. Welles uses space in an imaginative way. Sobriety is shown by empty spaces (the palace with its high vaults, the Boar's Head at the beginning), and celebration/drunkenness through spaces filled with people.

Welles varies the use of vertical stripes. At the beginning, in the woods, Falstaff can easily go through the black vertical trees. When the army is assembled for battle, the vertical pikes are a sign of strength, of protection. Finally, at Hal's crowning, the same pikes are a barrier, preventing Falstaff from getting to his King. This is also shown physically with the round Falstaff and the stick-like Henry IV.

The old men sit by the fire, like Major Amberson in *The Magnificent Ambersons*. In fact, all four elements play a part in the film. Fire for reflection. Water/snow for changes. Earth for death. Air for speed.

This is also a film about the battle between harsh rock (the austere palace, a product of technology) and soft wood (the friendly Boar's Head). All the fun scenes are acted out in natural places, and the battle represents technology invading the natural world.

The battle scene is an extraordinary achievement. Through a totally artificial style (speeded-up, slo-mo, abstract cutting, peculiar sounds) Welles manages to convey the brutality of conflict and its ultimate futility. People hack and slash at mud–soaked bodies so you cannot tell one side from the other. It took ten days to shoot, six weeks to edit together, and plays for six minutes. I suggest that it was a direct influence on the battle sequence in *Braveheart*, directed by second-unit maestro David Tomblin.

Audio Ideas: To complement the visual differences between the monarchy/technology and the peasants/nature, we have the aural equivalent with Gielgud's high-pitched mechanical tones and Welles' bass rotund rhythms. This is highlighted when Falstaff imitates Henry IV when role-playing with Hal. Symbolically, they switch roles – Hal becoming the King, as he will later in the story – taking on his father's voice. In the rejection scene at the end, Henry V, as he now is, has his father's voice.

On an odd note, I was amazed to find that Keith Baxter sounded exactly, and I mean exactly, like Kenneth Branagh. Now either this is a complete fluke or Branagh learned his English accent from this movie...

Themes: This is about the fall of Falstaff. He clings to his innocence – his one virtue – but is betrayed by Hal. When Falstaff finds out the truth, that Hal no longer loves him, he dies. The story within the story, a favourite Welles device (learned from Shakespeare), is when Hal and Falstaff put on a play in the Boar's Head.

Subtext: Welles is against the modern age and the vicious battle scenes show the end of chivalry and the rise of technology. Compare this to *The Magnificent Ambersons*, which is about the rise of the car, and *Citizen Kane*, which is about media and politics. Or *The Trial*, which is about the company man, specifically the kind of man employed by corporations like IBM. It is not that Welles dislikes technology per se (he loved innovating to make his films), but he is angered by the loss of integrity that seems to come with it.

Hal is the cold modern man. For all the love that Falstaff gives him, Hal plays the odds and decides, cynically, that he can get the kingdom. Henry IV believes that power must be won, not given, which is why he applauds Hotspur. Hotspur is a knight of old, like Falstaff – they are both part of *olde* England.

In some way, Hal has to make a journey similar to Georgie Minafer's in *The Magnificent Ambersons* – George had to choose between the ways of an honourable gentleman, or the ways of a common professional. In the end, by following the former course he is forced into the latter pattern, against his will. Here, Hal seems more calculating, as though he was enjoying himself with Falstaff, observing the machinations of the world, and picks his time to strike.

The tragedy of the movie is that Falstaff, who is a life-affirming good man, a rarity in fiction, undergoes a loss of innocence. He sees, for the first time, how cynical the person he loves has become and dies as a result, his heart broken. Hal represents the death of chivalry.

The film is about Hal deciding whether to follow his mentor, drunken Falstaff, or his father, sobering King Henry IV. It has been suggested that Welles' poignant portrayal came from personal experience – that drunken mentor Falstaff is Welles' alcoholic, fun-loving father, and that sober father Henry IV represents sober school mentor Skipper Hill. In his youth, Welles had rejected his father to try and reform him, but Richard Welles died before they met again. So, Hal's decision to reject Falstaff was also Welles'. Peculiarly, Welles' daughter Beatrice plays Falstaff's page, and bears witness to his death. Also, Silence had a stammer like the one Welles' brother Richard had. This is the sort of stuff biographers live for!

Background: Aged 15, Welles wrote *Five Kings* based on Shakespeare's plays *Henry IV Part I*, *Henry IV Part II*, *Henry V*, *Richard III* and *The Merry Wives of Windsor*, which told the story of Falstaff. Hilton Edwards wanted Welles to put on a play in Ireland to boost the coffers of Dublin's Gate Theatre, which at that time did not have a building to call its home. Welles wrote a new play from *Five Kings*, called it *Chimes at Midnight*, and opened in Belfast on 24 February 1960. It was neither a great success nor abject failure on its run in Dublin. Welles was generally pleased with the project and proceeded with part two of his plan – to film it.

First, after *Chimes at Midnight* closed in late March, Welles directed Laurence Olivier on stage in Ionesco's *Rhinoceros* and directed his film version of *The Trial*. Wanting to quickly follow up with another film, Welles was persuaded by producers Emiliano de la Piedras and Harry Saltzman to direct a film version of *Treasure Island*. Welles proposed to film it back-to-back with *Chimes at Midnight*, using the same locations, extras and crew, so that they got two films for their budget of $2.5 million. In fact, Welles thought it would be best to direct *Chimes at Midnight* first, as a sort of test film, and then proceed with the major production.

Working in his Madrid home, Welles designed the costumes and sets. To evoke Britain, he assembled British actors in the main roles. Filming began in September of 1964 in various locations around Spain: the Pyrenees, Sierra de Guadaramma, Cordova Castle and Madrid. They built only one set, the Boar's Head, in a garage, because it was much cheaper than building it in a studio. Welles designed, painted and blowtorched the set. He also designed the costumes, every one of which was stolen when filming ceased.

As with *Othello*, Welles had to make do with whatever he could get. Jeanne Moreau was only available for five days, so all the reverse shots where you do not see her face were performed by a double. John Gielgud had a much bigger part, but he was only around for ten days. They had a ruined church for seven days – Soria Cathedral – and it became the palace.

Technical difficulties plagued the film. Margaret Rutherford's wonderfully emotive speech upon Falstaff's death has a generator hum in the background. Welles was forced to use it because the performance is so good and she could not lipsync the speech with the same emotion. Also, the first ten minutes came back from the processors with the sound out of sync with the lips – alas, the producers did not have the money to repair the damage.

When it was obvious Welles could not meet his ten-month shooting schedule, producer Saltzman withdrew his distribution-deal money, stopping the shoot just before Christmas. Alfredo Matas came on board. Then in January 1965, Welles became ill with a serious gall bladder infection. After several weeks' rest and relaxation, he resumed filming. By this time, Piedras wanted work on *Treasure Island* to commence. To placate him, Welles sent Jesús Franco out to do scenery and non-essential shots. Years later John Hough was brought in to direct the film, which was released in 1973.

In March 1965, Welles received news that his mentor Dr Bernstein had died. Depressed, Welles did not leave his Madrid house for five days. Filming was completed in April 1965. Welles went to Paris to re-record voices and sound effects, edit the film and mix it. As usual, he dubbed the voices of several parts including Fernando Rey, messengers and certain grunts and groans in the battle scene.

Instead of having it ready for Cannes in May, Welles went off to do some acting work. The job of editing went on for the rest of 1965 and into the beginning of 1966. *Chimes at Midnight* was not submitted for Cannes until the following year, having its world premiere on 8 May 1966. The total cost was somewhere around $1.1 million.

Released in America in March 1967 to bad reviews, *Falstaff* (as it was retitled) was effectively ignored by both the public and critics. For example, a few years later an American producer said he wanted to offer Welles the part he was born to play: Falstaff. Welles did not know whether to laugh or cry.

The Verdict: This is Welles' favourite picture because he regards it as the least flawed. It is also the subject dearest to his heart. It is stunning in all departments: acting, photography, music, sets. Only some of the sound quality is at fault, but that is easily ignored. 5/5

The Immortal Story (1968)

'Everything I do today took me 25 years!'

Director & Writer: Orson Welles

Cast: Roger Coggio (Elishama Levinsky), Norman Eshley (Paul, The Sailor), Jeanne Moreau (Virginie Ducrot), Fernando Rey (Merchant), Orson Welles (Mr Charles Clay), 58mins

Alternative Titles: *The Hour of Truth*; *The Guinea Piece*

Background: Mr Clay, a wealthy merchant, hears the immortal story of a sailor who is paid to make love to an older woman. He takes it upon himself to turn the story into reality. Thus the enormous, old Mr Clay can vicariously enjoy the pleasure of power one last time. But the sailor and the woman have minds and emotions of their own.

Like Charles Foster Kane in *Citizen Kane*, Mr Clay is trying to play God, to make something happen. However, despite his wealth, there is something Clay cannot have – sex. This is about the impotence of power and how it affects both the person with the power and the people subject to it. So, like other Welles' movies, the themes include the fall of the big man, the fragility and abuse of power, a man caught in a web, and the loss of integrity.

Clay is surrounded by mirrors, which constantly remind him of his impotence. These are screens, like film or TV. Like Clay, we watch the lovers and live vicariously through them.

Welles claimed the story of the sailor paid to make love to a woman had actually been told to him on a tramp steamer. It was after this that he read the Isak Dinesen story and fell in love with her work. Whilst filming *Ferry to Hong Kong* (1959) in Hong Kong and Macao, Welles was stimulated by the location and began collecting art, vases, jade and lamps as props for a film based on the sailor's story. Welles had a $10,000 filming kit shipped to him – a portable camera, sound equipment and a lighting rig. During lulls in filming *Ferry to Hong Kong*, he assembled a crew and took shots of junks, streets, a Chinese funeral and buildings. Some of these shots were used in *The Immortal Story*.

In 1967, Welles persuaded French TV ORTF to finance an hour-long, limited-budget film of *The Immortal Story* in French, which they could show on the network. An English-language version would be completed for the UK/US market.

Welles set about filming in Paris and Madrid, beginning in September in the Parisian suburb of Rueil-Malmaison. After five weeks the production moved to Welles' house on the outskirts of Madrid, where the erotic scenes were done. They also shot in Cincon, a town outside Madrid, which doubled for Macao. When five more weeks had passed, the production moved to Budapest. The idea was that *The Immortal Story* would be part of an anthology of Dinesen stories. Welles began filming *The Deluge at Nordernay* under the title *The Heroine* with Oja Kodar, but the shoot wrapped on the first day when the producer proved to be insolvent. Another story, *A Country Tale*, starring Peter O'Toole, was planned but never started.

The Immortal Story premiered on French TV and in theatres on 24 May 1968 (Welles was dubbed by Philippe Noiret), and premiered in English at the New York Film Festival in the autumn of that year.

Welles said he had been in love with Danish novelist Isak Dinesen (real name Karen Blixen) for years. One time he went to Denmark to see her, stayed in a room for three days but could not summon the nerve to call her up. He spent four years writing her a love letter but she died before he finished it. His obsession with her work extended to writing a film script called *The Dreamers* based on one of her stories. Just before he died in 1985, Welles filmed and edited together 20 minutes of this script starring himself and Oja Kodar.

F for Fake (1973)

'Every true artist must, in his own way, be a magician, a charlatan.'

Director & Writer: Orson Welles

Cast: Orson Welles (Himself), Oja Kodar (The Girl), Joseph Cotten (Himself), François Reichenbach (Himself), Richard Wilson (Guest), Paul Stewart (Himself), Gary Graver (Himself), Peter Bogdanovich (Himself), William Alland (Himself), Laurence Harvey (Cameo), Clifford Irving (Himself), Nina Van Pallandt (Herself), Elmyr de Hory (Himself), 84 mins

Working Titles: *Vérités et Mensonges (Truth and Lies)*; *Question Mark*; *?*; *Fake*; *Hoax*

Story: This is an essay about an artist who forges art, and asks the questions, 'Can a forgery be a work of art?' and 'Are forgers artists in their own right?'

We begin with Welles performing magic tricks. 'A magician,' he informs us, 'is just an actor pretending to be a magician.' This is a film about lies but he promises that for the next hour he will tell the truth.

We are told the story of Elmyr de Hory and Clifford Irving, who both live in Ibiza. De Hory – he has had over 60 names – says he is not an actor. He explains that he could not make a living by selling his own art, so decided to copy the styles of Picasso and Matisse, selling them as authentic works. Could the faker be a fake? No. He draws a Matisse, then burns it. 'The art world is a huge confidence trick.' One museum has 22 post-Impressionist fakes and still thinks it has the real thing. Irving said that he had de Hory paint a Picasso and a Braque, took them to the Museum of Modern Art and had them authenticated within two hours.

Elmyr is a man of talent making the establishment look ridiculous. They claim to be experts in art, to be infallible and he exposes them by selling them fakes. The only reason Elmyr is not in jail is because of the embarrassment he could cause in the art world.

'It's pretty, but is it art?' It is all a matter of opinion. The expert is only one opinion – why should he decide what is good and bad? Who is the real faker? Michelangelo started work as a faker, smoking his work to make it look old.

Irving is a novelist whose writing did not sell, so he took to writing about de Hory in a book called *Fake*. Only Irving then wrote another book, about Howard Hughes, claiming to have met Hughes and read his diaries and papers. The papers were authenticated by experts. Then the voice of Hughes was broadcast, saying he had nothing to do with Irving. The truth was out, and Irving confessed, in another book.

Welles was also a faker – at the age of 16, he got his first acting role at the Gate Theatre by lying, saying that he was a great American actor on vacation. Furthermore, there was the night he panicked America with his infamous *The War of the Worlds* broadcast. Someone in South America tried the same trick and got put in jail – Welles got a Hollywood contract. Joseph Cotten and Richard Wilson explain that Welles was originally going to base *Citizen Kane* on Howard Hughes not William Randolph Hearst. There follows a *News on the March*, a newsreel for Howard Hughes, a skit on the one for Charles Foster Kane.

If there were no experts there would be no fakers.

De Hory could only be put in jail, under French law, if two people saw him sign a false name on the paintings. Does it matter? Does it matter that we know the name of the artist who made the art? We admire the great Chartres cathedral but the names of the artisans who made it will forever remain anonymous. A piece of art is a piece of art, regardless of who made it.

And for all we do, everything must die and disappear. 'Our songs will all be silent.'

Picasso – a movement of his hand on a piece of paper is worth more than gold. (The art market puts a monetary value on art, and applies an ego to the work that was never there.) There is a story that friends showed him pictures and, one by one, he dismissed them as fakes. 'But Pablo,' one of them said, 'I saw you draw this one.' Picasso said that he could paint false Picassos as well as anybody.

In Lucerne, years ago, there was a man under Picasso's window who always played the trombone, disturbing the great man. But, upon looking out, he spied a young Oja Kodar on the way to the beach. He spied her many times on her regular journeys to and from the beach and restaurants and wherever a young woman will roam. In his room, she posed for him. She inspired 22 paintings – 22 paintings she took for herself as payment for the days in the sun she missed.

Years later, during a foggy August in Paris, an exhibition is held of 22 canvases. Picasso is livid and travels there, and is even more angry to find them receiving great reviews. Arriving, he stares, in a rage, for none of them was painted by his hand. Oja takes Picasso to her grandfather, the world's greatest forger. They talk about art. (The story, and the conversation, are re-enacted by Welles and Kodar.) What is real art? And is art real? Humbly, the dying man says that Picasso changes from one style to another and, rather than copy, he decided to create a whole new period for Picasso. The originals? He burned them.

Welles pops up, announcing that he promised to tell the truth for an hour, and that that hour elapsed 17 minutes ago. Since then, he has been lying his head off. The truth is that they have been forging an art story.

'Art,' Welles concludes, 'is a lie which makes us see the truth.'

Visual Ideas: This is a scary film to watch because of the sheer scale of editing required to give the effects Welles required. We constantly move from one found image and sound to another – quickly, sharply. Words and images from different times and places are slotted together to make conversations and a cohesive narrative. At the time, this must have been quite shocking. Strangely, it now seems normal – the MTV generation has since experienced more extreme uses of mixed and sampled images, colours, sounds. If Stanley Kubrick used a mixture of styles in *A Clockwork Orange*, then Orson Welles used a mixture of media in *F for Fake*. Was Welles a precursor of MTV, and hence of Oliver Stone's *Natural Born Killers*? Although this cutting style is strange because it is found in media, it is not strange in the context of Welles – in a way, he used the same technique in *Citizen Kane*. When Charles, as a boy, says, 'Merry Christmas,' his guardian Thatcher replies, 'And a happy New Year!' in a reverse shot representing many years later. In this case, Welles was telling us a long time had passed. Ironically, in all films, each shot is filmed at a different time, sometimes at different places. In *Othello* there is a fight scene whose first blow was filmed in Africa, and whose second blow was filmed 2,000 miles away, yet we see it as continuous. Likewise, in *F for Fake*, we totally accept Welles' manipulation of time.

Audio Ideas: There are the usual explosions to wake us up, but also the silence with the raised eyebrow or a look.

Themes: Secrets. De Hory, Irving and Hughes all have secrets. We want to find out the truth, but does the truth matter? Man caught in a web: de Hory is portrayed as an ex-faker who has no money – all of the major money is made by the art dealers. The fragility of power: Hughes is seen sympathetically, if not pathetically.

Subtext: Welles delights in tricks. The film is a trick. He constantly tells us he is cheating, yet we believe the film. Even when he is showing us the film from Reichenbach's documentary, he then shows us Reichenbach, and even the film rolling on a moviola. This, above all, is a film about film trickery.

Welles plays magic tricks on children. Are we the children? When de Hory sells forgeries to art experts and millionaires, Welles is delighted. He is pricking a balloon, showing that money and knowledge – two things the world prizes beyond reason – are not important.

There is a relationship between de Hory and Irving that smacks of other previous male bondings in Welles' films, but we do not know who is the man of power in the pair.

De Hory is constantly trying to make money to stay alive. Does Welles identify with him?

Of course Pauline Kael accused Welles of being a charlatan, a faker, an art thief, a fraud, a man who had fooled the experts into believing he had made a film called *Citizen Kane*. Is this film Welles' reply? Two moments are telling. First, Welles says that the work of art itself is important – the fact that it exists – not the person who made it. Secondly, eventually, it will all turn to dust.

Background: In 1970, Charles Higham wrote a biography suggesting that Welles was afraid of finishing films and the following year, in the *New Yorker* and a preface to *The Citizen Kane Book*, Pauline Kael launched an attack on Welles' authorship of *Citizen Kane*, saying that Herman J Mankiewicz was the sole author. John Houseman's memoirs were also derogatory towards Welles. Welles was deeply hurt by these public humiliations and was brought to tears. His lawyer advised against suing Kael – the book remains available as a result – and instead Welles tried to refute his critics by simply finishing a movie.

In 1972, hoping to reduce his enormous tax bill, Welles decided to assemble a television film about Elmyr de Hory, the famous art forger, who had been the subject of the book *Fake* by Clifford Irving. They had both been interviewed for a BBC documentary by François Reichenbach. Welles negotiated for the rights to all the footage Reichenbach shot, including the out-takes. Reichenbach provided Welles with an editing room in Paris. Work progressed and, as Welles was putting the finishing touches to the TV film, the news came in that Clifford Irving had falsely claimed to have interviewed Howard Hughes for his unauthorised Hughes biography. Welles now had two fakers in his programme, not one. In an instant, he decided that he should turn his programme into a feature film, dividing the time between three charlatans: de Hory, Irving and Welles.

(Many years previously, Welles had worked on an abortive project, another mixture of documentary footage and fiction called *It's All True*, to which the title of this film is perhaps an ironic allusion.)

They worked seven days a week in three editing rooms for a full year putting the film together. Welles was bursting with energy. Work was completed late summer of 1973 and it premiered September 1974 at film festivals in New York and San Sebastian. The commercial failure of *F for Fake* was a shock to Welles, who thought that the personal essay was a new format that would find favour with the masses. De Hory committed suicide a few years later.

The Verdict: This is a lively, inventive film that darts from whimsy to anguish to thoughts of mortality with ease. It is a genuine original. Would I lie to you? 4/5

Filming Othello (1978)

'My definition of success is not having things
thrown at me!'

Director & Writer: Orson Welles

Cast: Orson Welles (Himself), Micheál MacLiammóir
(Himself), Hilton Edwards (Himself), 90 mins

Story: The film consists of Welles in front of a moviola,
talking to the camera. He explains the ideas behind the
making of his 1952 film *Othello*, which are most revealing.
Inserted are an interview with Hilton Edwards and
Micheál MacLiammóir, and a question and answer session
with an audience in Boston.

Background: In 1974 a German TV station approached
Welles – they wanted to show *Othello* on German television, and thought a companion piece by Welles about the
making of it would be nice. Taking their idea, but using his
own money, Welles began by shooting an interview with
Hilton Edwards and Micheál MacLiammóir in a Paris
hotel. (Instead of doing the reverse shots then and there,
Welles filmed them two years later, echoing the way the

original film was made.)

Welles made up storyboards then went to Dublin to film Micheál and Hilton at their house and at the Gate Theatre. He went on to Venice, and did about an hour of footage riding through the canals, pointing out the locations where *Othello* was filmed. A further trip to Morocco was planned but did not materialise. Then the negative of the location footage disappeared. (A brief glimpse can be seen in Gary Graver's documentary, *Working With Orson Welles*.)

After working on *The Other Side of the Wind*, Welles wrote a script and resumed working on *Filming Othello* in 1976. He shot his narration in the living room of his Beverly Hills house and finished it in 1977. *Filming Othello* premiered at the Berlin Film Festival in June of 1978 and ran for three weeks in one New York cinema in 1979.

Welles enjoyed making *Filming Othello*, so in 1981 he began work on a follow-up, *Filming The Trial*, which was never completed.

Lost Films

'Sour Grapes is Not my Dish'

When Orson Welles died on 10 October 1985, he left behind a seemingly endless number of scripts, and films he began shooting but never finished through lack of finance. Here is a selection of what–might–have–beens:

It's All True (1993)

Working Title: *Pan-American*

Background: 1941. Welles was asked (not by Nelson Rockefeller as is often stated) to make a propaganda film cementing USA/Latin American relations during World War Two. The idea was that by making a film in Mexico, Brazil and America, it would show that they were one happy continent and all anti-Nazi. Welles loved Rio de Janeiro and filmed everything from weird and wonderful angles. There were two problems. First, his absence in Brazil allowed RKO to re-edit *The Magnificent Ambersons* without him. Second, although he shot all the film, by the time he returned to Hollywood RKO refused to put up more money for Welles to edit it together. Welles used his fee from acting in *Jane Eyre* to develop the film, but in 1946 forfeited the film and all rights to RKO and a businessman.

This reconstruction begins with a background documentary, then there are snippets of the first two parts (*My Friend Bonito* shot in Mexico by Norman Foster, and colour footage of a Rio carnival) and virtually all of Welles silent *Four Men on a Raft*, about four peasant fishermen's 1,650-mile sea voyage to the Brazilian fascist leader, Vargas, to protest about their atrocious living and working conditions. It is simplistic propaganda, stunningly filmed, but a curio nonetheless. This documentary/essay form is one he would later use for *F for Fake* and *Filming Othello*.

Don Quixote (1992)

Background: Welles began filming in 1957 and continued filming around Europe for many years. Boxes of edited film were scattered all over the world. Stories about the filming have taken on a legendary quality but, although much editing was done (Welles cut it to the rhythm of his own reading of the script), Welles could not complete it. Fed up with people asking about it, Welles announced he was going to release it as a personal essay about Spain called *Whatever Happened to Don Quixote?* In 1992, under the supervision of Welles' companion Oja Kodar, it was finished by Jesús Franco and Patxi Irigoyen. It fails to capture the spirit/style/rhythm of Welles.

The Deep (1970)

Background: Also known as *Dead Reckoning*, this film is based on the excellent thriller *Dead Calm* by Charles Williams. It follows the novel more closely than the later Philip Noyce film starring Sam Neill, Nicole Kidman and Billy Zane. Filmed from 1967 to 1969 in Yugoslavia, Jeanne Moreau and others said that this was essentially completed. Welles said that two scenes were missing which required the late Laurence Harvey.

The Other Side of the Wind (1980)

Working Title: *The Sacred Beasts*

Background: Filmed in the houses of friends, or by illegally sneaking into film studios, it is the story of maverick film director JJ Jake Hannaford (John Huston), who returns to Hollywood in a blaze of publicity. He puts aside his morals and artistic sensibilities to make a purely commercial film full of sex and violence. Obviously a play on Welles' image, as well as other people's image of him, the scenes I have seen look stunning and vintage Welles. It was completed but, due to legal difficulties involving the brother of the Shah of Iran and the Iranian revolutionaries, it has remained under lock and key in Paris. Every so often rumours persist of its imminent release.

Resource Materials

'He was some kind of a man. What does it matter what
you say about people?'
— Tanya (*Touch of Evil*, 1958)

Books

Anderegg, Michael, *Orson Welles, Shakespeare and Popular
Culture*, Columbia University Press, 1999

Bazin, André, *Orson Welles*, Harper and Row, 1978

Benamou, Catherine, *It's All True: Orson Welles's Pan-
American Odyssey*, University of California Press, 2007

Beja, Morris, ed., *Perspectives on Orson Welles*, GK Hall, 1995

Berg, Chuck and Erskine, Tom, eds., *The Encyclopedia of
Orson Welles*, Checkmark Books, 2003

Berthomé, Jean-Pierre and François Thomas, *Orson Welles
at Work*, Phaidon, 2008

Bessy, Maurice, *Orson Welles: An investigation into his films
and philosophy*, Crown, 1971

Callow, Simon, *Orson Welles: The Road to Xanadu*, Viking,
1996

Callow, Simon, *Orson Welles: Hello Americans*, Viking, 2006

Carringer, Robert, *The Making of Citizen Kane*, University
of California Press, 1985

Carringer, Robert, *The Magnificent Ambersons: A Reconstruction*, University of California Press, 1993

Comito, Terry, ed., *Touch of Evil*, Rutgers, 1985

Conrad, Peter, *Orson Welles: The Stories of His Life*, Faber and Faber, 2003

Cowie, Peter, *The Cinema of Orson Welles*, Da Capo Press, 1973

Davies, Anthony, *Filming Shakespeare's Plays*, Cambridge University Press, 1988

Drazin, Charles, *In Search of the Third Man*, Limelight, 2000

Drössler, Stefan, ed., *The Unknown Orson Welles*, Filmmuseum München, 2004

Estrin, Mark, ed., *Orson Welles Interviews*, University Press of Mississippi, 2002

Feder, Chris Welles, *The Movie Director*, privately published, 2002

Feeney, FX, (Paul Duncan, ed.), *Orson Welles*, Taschen, 2006

France, Richard, ed., *Orson Welles on Shakespeare*, Routledge, 2001

France, Richard, *The Theatre of Orson Welles*, Bucknell University Press, 1977

Garis, Robert, *The Films of Orson Welles*, Cambridge University Press, 2004

Gottesman, Ronald, ed., *Focus on Citizen Kane*, Prentice Hall, 1971

Gottesman, Ronald, ed., *Focus on Orson Welles*, Prentice Hall, 1976

Greene, Graham, *The Third Man*, Faber and Faber, 1991

Heyer, Paul, *The Medium and the Magician: Orson Welles, The*

Radio Years, Rowman and Littlefield, 2005

Heylin, Clinton, *Despite the System: Orson Welles Versus the Hollywood Studios*, Chicago Review Press, 2005

Higham, Charles, *Orson Welles: The Rise and Fall of an American Genius*, St. Martin's Press, 1985. Higham presents Welles as the instigator of his own downfall, saying that Welles did not complete his films because he had a directing version of stage fright, and an anti-commercial standpoint. If something bad happens, then nine times out of ten Welles is to blame. (Higham wrote a book on Welles in 1970, which put forth the same opinion – Welles disliked it intensely, and went so far as to feature a disparaging caricature of Higham in the character Higgam, who appears in *The Other Side of the Wind*.) To his credit, Higham has done his biographical research and disproves many Wellesian childhood myths. Also, Higham puts forward interesting psychological theories, some of which may be accurate.

Howard, James, *The Complete Films of Orson Welles*, Citadel Press, 1991

Jorgens, Jack J, *Shakespeare on Film*, Indiana University Press, 1977

Kael, Pauline, Herman J Mankiewicz and Orson Welles, *The Citizen Kane Book*, Bantam, 1971

Leaming, Barbara, *Orson Welles*, Viking, 1985. Imagine, if you will, visiting Welles every day for a cosy luncheon and being bombarded with anecdotes and tangential ideas and movie gossip and opinions. Well, here is over 600 pages of it, backed up with lots of firsthand interviews. It portrays Welles in a positive light and really brings across what great fun he was. This is probably your best starting-point to learn about Welles in more detail.

Lebo, Harlan, *Citizen Kane: The Fiftieth Anniversary Album*, Doubleday, 1990

Lyons, Bridget Gellert, ed., *Chimes at Midnight*, Rutgers, 1988

MacLiammóir, Micháel, *Put Money in Thy Purse: The Filming of Orson Welles' Othello*, Methuen, 1952

McBride, Joseph, *Whatever Happened to Orson Welles? A Portrait of an Independent Career*, University Press of Kentucky, 2006

Mulvey, Laura, *Citizen Kane*, BFI, 1992

Naremore, James, *The Magic World of Orson Welles*, Southern Methodist University Press, 1989

Naremore, James, ed., *Orson Welles's Citizen Kane: A Casebook*, Oxford University Press, 2004

Noble, Peter, *The Fabulous Orson Welles*, Hutchinson, 1956

Perkins, VF, *The Magnificent Ambersons*, BFI, 1999

Rosenbaum, Jonathan, *Discovering Orson Welles*, University of California Press, 2007

Taylor, John Russell, *Orson Welles: A Celebration*, Pavilion, 1986

Thieme, Cynthia, *F for Fake and the Growth in Complexity of Orson Welles's Documentary Form*, Peter Lang, 1997

Thomson, David, *Rosebud: The Story of Orson Welles*, Alfred A Knopf, 1996

Tonguette, Peter Prescott, *Orson Welles Remembered: Interviews with his Actors, Editors, Cinematographers and Magicians*, McFarland, 2007

Walsh, John Evangelist, *Walking Shadows: Orson Welles, William Randolph Hearst and Citizen Kane*, The University of Wisconsin Press, 2004

Walters, Ben, *Welles*, Haus, 2004

Welles, Orson, *Everybody's Shakespeare*, The Toad Press, 1934

Welles, Orson (Serge Greffet trans.), *Miracle à Hollywood & À bon entendeur* [*The Unthinking Lobster & Fair Warning*], Un table ronde, 1952

Welles, Orson (Maurice Bessy trans.), *Une grosse legume*, Gallimard, 1953

Welles, Orson, *Mr Arkadin*, WH Allen, 1954

Welles, Orson, *Moby Dick-Rehearsed: A Drama in Two Acts*, Samuel French, 1965

Welles, Orson and Oja Kodar, *The Big Brass Ring*, Black Spring Press, 1991

Welles, Orson, *The Cradle Will Rock*, Santa Teresa Press, 1994

Welles, Orson, *Les Bravades*, Workman, 1996

Welles, Orson and Bogdanovich, Peter (edited by Jonathan Rosenbaum), *This is Orson Welles*, Da Capo Press, 1998. From 1969 to 1972 Bogdanovich interviewed Welles eight times in various places around Europe and America. Then, for various reasons, the project could not be completed. Twenty years later, it was published. And the verdict? Brilliant. Bogdanovich is a shrewd questioner, and Welles is wary of giving too much away and is constantly trying to change the subject. Despite the evasion, Welles explains his thinking behind many of the films. In addition, there is a lengthy chronology, and the screenplay of the missing pieces of *The Magnificent Ambersons*. This has also been released on audio that you should really track down.

Welles, Orson and Oja Kodar, *The Other Side of the Wind*,

Cahiers du cinéma/Festival International du Film de Locarno, 2005

White, Rob, *The Third Man*, BFI, 2003

Wood, Bret, *Orson Welles: A Bio-Bibliography*, Greenwood Blue, 1990

Websites

Wellesnet – http://www.wellesnet.com/ – Sometimes opinionated, but completely essential for all Welles fans. As well as news on the latest books and films, there are many video, radio and text links to keep you listening, watching and reading Welles for the next decade or two.

Index

academics, 14
Adventures of Harry Lime, The, 96
advertising, 14, 109
Advocate, 114, 116–117, 119–121, 124–125
aliens, 15
Anders, Glenn, 59, 65, 68
Arden, Robert, 88, 97, 99
Arkadin, 19–20, 88–99
Around the World in Eighty Days, 58, 65
art, 20–21, 38, 43, 124, 136, 138–144
artist, 13, 16, 41, 117–118, 138, 140
Auer, Mischa, 88, 98
Austerlitz, 122

Badge of Evil, 100, 106–107
battle, 70, 75, 127, 129, 130, 134
Baxter, Anne, 44, 50
Baxter, Keith, 126, 130
Bernstein, Dr, 21, 27, 40, 133
Bessy, Maurice, 98
Big Brass Ring, The, 12
Black Magic, 75–76, 82
Black Prince, The, 83
Blitzstein, Marc, 12
Brighton Rock, 105
Britain, 27, 132
broadcast, 28, 37, 49, 139–140
budget, 38–39, 42, 49, 57, 68, 73, 75, 107–108, 123, 132, 136
business, 20, 32, 40, 43, 45, 50, 58, 122

Cabinet of Dr Caligari, The, 93
Cannes, 12, 87, 134
Castle, William, 65–66
censorship, 38
Charles Foster Kane, 19, 21, 30–31, 135, 140
Chimes at Midnight, 29, 47, 126, 132, 134
chivalry, 130–131
Chronicle, The, 32, 35
Chronicles of England Scotlande and Irelande, 25
Citizen Kane, 11–13, 19, 28–30, 38, 40, 42–43, 48, 51, 130, 135, 140, 142–143
Citizen Welles, 40
classics, 24
Cloutier, Suzanne, 78, 85
Coen, Frankie, 111
Cohn, Harry, 57, 65, 73
Collins, Ray, 18, 30, 44, 50, 100
commercials, 15
Compulsion, 23
Coote, Robert, 78, 83, 87
costumes, 18, 65, 74–75, 84, 132
Cotten, Joseph, 30, 38–39, 42, 44, 78, 85, 100, 107, 138, 140
Country Tale, A, 137
Cradle Will Rock, 12, 22
critics, 14, 17, 51, 113, 125, 134, 144
Crowd, The, 119
Curtiss, Edward, 110

de Corsica, Ted, 18, 59
de Hory, Elmyr, 138–139, 144

Dead Calm, 150
death, 19–22, 36, 41–42, 48, 56, 71, 81, 89, 93, 106, 110, 114, 121, 123–124, 128–131, 133
deep focus, 17
Deep, The, 150
Desdemona, 78–86
dialogue, 16–18, 23–24, 41, 47, 63, 81, 97, 105, 111, 125
Dietrich, Marlene, 100, 107, 109
Dinesen, Isak, 136–137
directing, 14–15, 52, 76
Doctor Faustus, 17, 22
Dolivet, Louis, 96, 98
Don Quixote, 149
Dowling, Doris, 78, 84
Dreamers, The, 137

editing, 42, 50, 57, 73, 75, 87, 93, 97–98, 104, 110, 112, 124, 134, 141, 144, 149–150
Edwards, Hilton, 13, 26, 78, 83, 96, 132, 146
Eisenstein, Sergei, 71–72, 93
Elsa Bannister, 19, 59
emotions, 23, 120, 135
Europe, 22, 27, 32, 37, 46, 49, 90, 97, 112, 149
Expressionism, 17

F for Fake, 20, 28, 138, 142, 144, 149
Falstaff, 20, 47, 126–134
Ferry to Hong Kong, 136
Fier, Jack, 67
Filming Othello, 18, 147
finance, 14, 27, 49, 58, 83, 136, 148
financing, 16, 82, 84
Five Kings, 131–132
Fleck, Freddie, 50
Flynn, Errol, 65–66, 96
Fontaine, Joan, 78, 85
fortune, 31, 48, 89–90
Foster, Norman, 50, 149
Franco, Jesús, 133, 149

Gabor, Zsa Zsa, 100, 107
Gance, Abel, 122
Gare d'Orsay, 124
George Minafer, 19–20, 47–49, 131

Gielgud, John, 126, 133
Gilda, 65, 67
Godfather, The, 23
Goetz, William, 57
Greek Meets Greek, 96
guilt, 55, 70, 121

Hank Quinlan, 20, 100–101
Hayworth, Rita, 59, 65, 83
Hearst, William Randolph, 12, 40–43, 140
Heart of Darkness, 39
Hearts of Age, 38
Heston, Charlton, 100, 106–107
Hickenlooper, George, 12
Higham, Charles, 143
Hitchcock, Alfred, 109
Hitler, Adolf, 43
Holinshed, Raphael, 25
Hollywood, 11, 16, 22, 26, 28, 38–39, 52, 57, 65, 67–68, 73, 75–76, 82, 108, 110, 140, 148, 150
Holt, Tom, 50
Hough, John, 133
House, Billy, 53, 57–58
Houseman, John, 17, 21, 40, 143
Hughes, Howard, 39, 139–140, 144
Huston, Walter, 49
Huxley, Aldous, 107

Iago, 19–20, 78–87
If I Die Before I Wake, 64–65
Immortal Story, The, 135–137
independent, 16, 28
innocence, 19, 36–37, 57, 93, 121, 130–131
Inquirer, The, 32, 35, 41
Inspector General, The, 26
Insull, Samuel, 39
Irving, Clifford, 138–139, 144
It's All True, 50, 144, 148
Ivan the Terrible, 71–72, 93

Jane Eyre, 23, 149
Jedediah Leland, 30, 33, 40
Jew Süss, 26
Journey Into Fear, 50
Julius Caesar, 22, 86

Kael, Pauline, 143
Kafka, Franz, 121–124
Keller, Harry, 111
King Lear, 24–25
King, Sherwood, 64
Koch, Howard, 28
Kodar, Oja, 12, 123, 137–138, 140, 149
Kubrick, Stanley, 142

labyrinth, 13, 29–30, 118
Lady from Shanghai, The, 59, 68, 71, 73
Lady in the Ice, The, 18
Lang, Fritz, 109
Law, 114, 118, 124
Lawrence, Viola, 67
Leigh, Janet, 100, 107, 109
lighting, 17, 23, 35, 77, 118, 136
location, 26, 66, 82, 107, 136, 147
Lucidi, Renzo, 98
Lynch, David, 52, 105

Macbeth, 19, 56, 69–76
MacLeish, Archibald, 21
MacLiammóir, Michael, 26, 78, 82–87, 96, 146
Madame Butterfly, 23
magicians, 15, 50, 138
Magnificent Ambersons, The, 17, 21, 29, 44, 48–51, 129–131, 148
Man in the Shadow, 107
Mankiewicz, Herman J, 12, 30, 39–41, 143
Mankowitz, Wolf, 98
March of Time, The, 17
Masterson, Whit, 106
McCambridge, Mercedes, 100, 107
Menzies, Pete, 100–101, 105
Mercury Theatre, 22, 28, 42, 49
Metty, Russell, 56, 108
Michael O'Hara, 19, 59
Midsummer Night's Dream, A, 25
Miller, George, 81
Moby Dick, 24
money, 11, 14, 23, 28, 37–38, 46–48, 51–53, 60, 65, 68, 75, 83–87, 91–95, 97 –98, 109, 112,

117, 121–122, 124, 127, 133, 142–143, 146, 148
Moorehead, Agnes, 17, 30, 44, 57
Moreau, Jeanne, 114, 126, 133, 135, 150
Morgan, JP, 40
Mori, Paola, 88, 96, 99, 114
Moss, Jack, 50
moviola, 18, 143, 146
Mr Arkadin, 19, 88, 99
Muhl, Eddie, 106, 110
Murch, Walter, 13
Murder My Sweet/ Farewell, My Lovely, 63
Murphy, Charles W, 40
music, 47, 68, 104–105, 134
My Friend Bonito, 149

nature, 26, 64, 88, 94–95, 129
New York, 12, 17, 26, 40, 42, 59, 73, 87, 98, 125, 137, 144, 147
News on the March, 28, 30–31, 36, 42, 140
newsreel, 36–37, 42, 140
Nims, Ernest, 57, 110
Noiret, Philippe, 137
Nolan, Jeanette, 18, 69, 74

O'Brady, Frederick, 96
O'Toole, Peter, 137
oppression, 122
Oscars, 11, 51, 65, 88, 91–92
Othello, 15, 19–20, 27, 29, 73, 75–76, 78–87, 125, 133, 142, 146–147, 149
Other Side of the Wind, The, 15, 147, 150

Panic!, 21
Perkins, Anthony, 114, 125
photography, 17, 52, 56, 74, 110, 128, 134
Picasso, 139–141
Piedras, Emiliano de la, 132
politics, 21, 122, 130
power, 19–20, 22, 33, 36, 38, 47, 49, 64, 69–70, 72, 79, 82, 93–94, 117, 120–122, 130, 135–136, 142–143
producing, 15

radio, 14–15, 17, 27–29, 31, 42, 49, 74, 92, 96–97
Reed, Carol, 24, 83, 97
Reichenbach, François, 138, 144
Republic Pictures, 73
Rey, Fernando, 126, 134–135
RKO, 12–13, 37–39, 41–42, 48–51, 148–149
Robbins, Tim, 12
Robinson, Edward G, 53, 57
Rosebud, 19, 30–32, 34–36, 41
Ross, Benjamin, 12
Rutherford, Margaret, 126, 133

Salkind, Alexander and Michael, 122
Saltzman, Harry, 132
San Simeon, 40–41
Scalera, Montatori, 82
script, 26, 40–41, 50, 57, 65, 75, 96, 106–109, 123, 137, 147, 149
sex, 135, 150
Shadow, The, 27
Shaefer, George, 38–39, 49
Shakespeare, William, 24–26, 73, 77, 82–83, 130–131
sketch, 18, 93
Smiler With a Knife, 39
Spiegel, Sam, 57
Stein, Cliff, 111
Stell, Aaron, 110
Stevens, Ashton, 40
Stewart, Paul, 18, 30, 138
Stone, Oliver, 142
story, 18, 21, 33–34, 39, 41–42, 48–49, 52, 58, 63–64, 76, 82–83, 89, 92, 94 –98, 121, 127, 130, 132, 135–141, 150
storyboards, 50, 147
Stranger, The, 6, 53, 57–58, 110
studio, 15–16, 37–38, 41, 67–68, 107–109, 112, 132
suicide, 21, 34, 95, 145

Tamiroff, Akim, 88, 99–100, 110, 114
theatre, 12, 14–17, 25–26, 42, 50, 58, 62, 65, 116
Third Man, The, 23, 56, 83, 96
To Have and Have, 63
Todd School, 25
Toland, Gregg, 30, 35, 42
Too Much Johnson, 38
totalitarian state, 39, 122
Touch of Evil, 13, 19, 29, 56, 81, 100, 105, 112–113
Treasure Island, 132–133
Trial, The, 13, 29, 105, 114, 120–125, 130, 132, 147

unions, 12, 67, 78, 107

Van Stratten, 20, 88–96, 99
Veiller, Anthony, 57
Venice Film Festival, 76
Vidor, King, 49, 119
voiceover, 18, 47, 63, 72

Walker, Vernon, 50
Walter Parks Thatcher 30–32, 35, 37, 40, 142
War of the Worlds, The, 28, 37, 140
Wayne, John, 75
Weaver, Dennis, 100, 109
Wilson, Richard, 73, 75–76, 138, 140
Wise, Robert, 42, 50
writing, 14–15, 25, 41, 64, 96, 123, 137, 139
Wynn, Keenan, 100, 107

Xanadu, 31, 34–35, 41

Yates, Herbert J, 75
Young, Loretta, 53, 57

Zouk, Jakob, 88–89, 92, 99
Zugsmith, Albert, 106